Charles Wenyon

Across Siberia

On the great post-road

Charles Wenyon

Across Siberia
On the great post-road

ISBN/EAN: 9783337254100

Printed in Europe, USA, Canada, Australia, Japan

Cover: Foto ©Andreas Hilbeck / pixelio.de

More available books at **www.hansebooks.com**

ACROSS SIBERIA

ACROSS SIBERIA

ON THE GREAT POST-ROAD

BY

CHARLES WENYON, M.D.

London:
CHARLES H. KELLY
2, CASTLE ST., CITY RD.; AND 66, PATERNOSTER ROW, E.C.
1896

To

My Wife

PREFACE

HE old post-roads of England have been superseded by the railway, and the same fate will soon befall the great post-road of Siberia. Within the last two years an important section of the Trans-Siberian railway has been opened for traffic, and I was perhaps one of the last Englishmen to travel the whole distance from the Pacific coast to the Ural Mountains in the old-fashioned way. The following sketch, therefore, of a journey made from China to Europe through Northern Asia in the spring and summer of 1893 is partly a record of circumstances which have passed or are fast passing away.

CHARLES WENYON.

CANTON, CHINA, 1896.

CONTENTS

CHAPTER I
OFF THE SIBERIAN COAST

Crowded deck—Navvies for Siberian Railway—Chinese gamblers—Fight for food 3

CHAPTER II
THE EASTERN TERMINUS

Harbour and town of Vladivostock—Mixed population—German merchants—A Siberian Sebastopol—Argus-eyed police . . 8

CHAPTER III
THE GREAT POST-ROAD

An immense country—Diversified configuration—Track of early settlers—The Great Plateau—Alpine ranges—Rigorous climate—Sparse population—Modes of travel—Post-horse system . . 16

CHAPTER IV
THE START

A traveller's narrative—Presentiments—A wintry day—Turning back—A royal traveller—Appalling distances—Poor accommodation—Monotony—The sort of people to enjoy it . . . 22

CHAPTER V
FROM THE COAST TO LAKE KHANKA, BY TARANTASS

First post-station—Attempted extortion—Lonely country—A Siberian graveyard—Heating apparatus—A night in the travellers' room—Noisy company—Description of a tarantass—Russian horses—Use of pillows—Corduroy bridges and roads—Fast driving—Stuck in a bog 28

CHAPTER VI

LIFE IN A SIBERIAN VILLAGE

A post-road of ice—Crossing Khanka in a sledge—Waiting for a thaw—Kamenrubeloff—A Russian land-surveyor—Our lodgings—A small dinner-party—Washing—Siberian peasants—Extension of Russian territory—Cossacks—Gipsies—Music—The church and its services—Sacrament of Lord's Supper—St. George's day—Contentment of villagers—A wedding—Clouds in the sky 49

CHAPTER VII

BY STEAMER FROM KHANKA TO THE AMOOR

Crossing Khanka lake — Sungacha river — Wild ducks — Fellow-passengers—Tea and vodka—"Siberian wives"—A drunken engineer—Usuri river—Fish-skin Tartars—*Yukola*—Shamanism—Sable-hunting—Khabarofka—Russia and Cathay—Cathedral—Martial music 71

CHAPTER VIII

UP THE AMOOR

Confluence with the Usuri—A set of gamblers—Baccarat—Flowery hillsides—Salmon—Anglers—Blagovestchensk—Gold-mining on Zeya river—Russian defence of frontier—Apathy of China—Sociability of Russian people—Military officers—Jews—Deck passengers—Priests, emigrants, and soldiers—Wood-stations—Purchase of provisions—Wild scenery—Night on the river—Forest fires—Men overboard — Shilka and Argun rivers — Stretensk 92

CHAPTER IX

FROM STRETENSK TO LAKE BAIKAL, BY TARANTASS

Crossing the Shilka—A Telyega ride—In the wrong house—Nertchinsk and Kara—The higher terrace of the plateau—Cold nights—Tchita—Raft-building—Dry climate—Exiled Socialists—An English resident—At a picnic—Prince Datpak—The Tungus—On the Buriat steppe—Trinity Sunday—Drunkenness and worship—The Buriats—Popootchiks—Verchni-Udinsk—Russian lovers'—Signboards — Raskolniks — Summer flowers—

Selenga River—Trout-streams—Approaching Baikal—The lake—
Its size and loneliness—The post-station on the shore—An
unamiable wife — An overcrowded lodging-house — Fish and
flowers   117

CHAPTER X

THROUGH IRKUTSK TO TOMSK, BY TARANTASS

Distant view of Irkutsk—Its wealth and public institutions—The
taiga—Not so deserted as it seems—Bears and wolves—Alone in
the forest—Caravans—Exiles going east: criminal, political, and
religious—Penalties of dissent—Strange sects—Treatment of
exiles on the road—Irregularities—Convict stations—Attempts
to escape—*Bradyaga*—Diseases of Siberia—Cholera—Hiring
outside horses—Out in a thunderstorm—Crossing the Yenisei—
Krasnoiarsk—Atchinsk—Cheap horses and provisions—Tartars
—Samoyedes—The last stage on the post-road   .   .   .   161

CHAPTER XI

FROM TOMSK TO THE URAL MOUNTAINS, BY RIVER AND RAILWAY

The city and government of Tomsk—On the Obi—Rafts—A camp
of Ostiaks—Russian methods of evangelism—Long days—The
Irtish river—The Tobol and the city of Tobolsk—Fertile
plains—The great northern swamps—Mammoth remains—
Religious refugees—Russian undergraduates—Confluences of
Siberian rivers—The Toora river and city of Tiumen—On the
railway — Ural Mountains scenery — Ekaterinburg — "Europe"
and "Asia"   201

CHAPTER XII

CROSSING THE RUSSIAN FRONTIER

Suspicious of strangers—Heterogeneous population—Difficulty of
government — Detectives at frontier station — Detained on
suspicion—The village of Wirballen—The frontier line—Russian
and German sentinels—Out of the cage at last   .   .   .   233

LIST OF ILLUSTRATIONS

	PAGE
PORTRAIT	*Frontispiece*
MAP	*to face* 1
CHINESE FIGHTING FOR RICE	2
VLADIVOSTOCK	9
A POST-HOUSE STATION	29
OUR TARANTASS	39
FAST DRIVING	43
LOG-HOUSE	52
ON THE AMOOR	95
THE SHILKA RIVER AND THE TOWN OF STRETENSK	116
NERTCHINSK	123
TCHITA	129
TUNGU	133
SELENGA RIVER AND VALLEY	151
LAKE BAIKAL, AND STEAMER LANDING	161
THE MUSEUM, IRKUTSK	164
THE CATHEDRAL, IRKUTSK	165
A PARTY OF EXILES CROSSING THE YENISEI	171
THE CATHEDRAL, KRASNOIARSK	192
TARTAR OR TATA	196
SAMOYEDE ENCAMPMENT	197
EXILES	200
PART OF THE MARKET SQUARE, TOMSK	203
STEAMER TOWING BARGE	207
TODOLSK	215
A STREET IN EKATERINBURG	227
THE SIBERIAN BOUNDARY POST	231

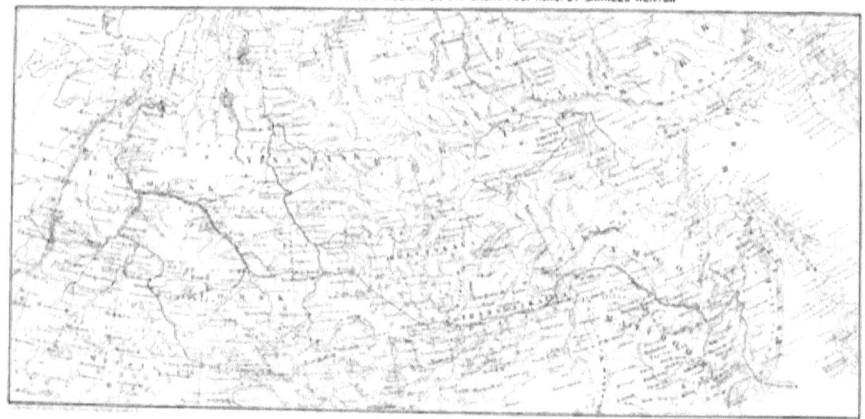

ROUTE MAP TO ILLUSTRATE 'ACROSS SIBERIA' ON THE GREAT POST ROAD. BY CHARLES WENYON

CHINESE FIGHTING FOR RICE.

ACROSS SIBERIA

CHAPTER I

OFF THE SIBERIAN COAST

E are nearing Vladivostock," said the captain, and the only European passenger was very glad to hear it.

To think of reaching port always gives a thrill of pleasure even on the happiest voyage, and it naturally gave a deeper thrill to one who had endured the misery of a voyage such as this. In some respects it could not have been more favourable,—calm sea and cloudless sky, a well-found ship, obliging officers, and a quick run of twelve days from the China coast, including a stay of thirty hours at Nagasaki,—but the crowd of passengers we had on board spoiled everything.

Those who have travelled by excursion steamers on the English coast perhaps know something about crowded decks; but between living in a crowd for a few hours and living in one for twice as many days, there is a vast difference; and there is still a vaster difference between a crowd of English lads and lasses and such a crowd as ours.

It all came about through the restless enterprise of the Russian Government, which, not content with its great highroad through Siberia, must now seek to supersede it by a railway. The eastern section—a stretch of about two hundred miles, from the coast to the Usuri River—had already been commenced; but, all the European labour available not being sufficient for the work, the officials had at last decided to import ten thousand Chinese coolies to complete it.

The first gang of eleven hundred were shipped by the steamer on which I had the misfortune to be a passenger. She was not a large vessel, and with five hundred persons on board would have been uncomfortably crowded; having more than twice that number, the decks were literally covered with them, and outside the cabin there was hardly room to move.

The crush was no inconvenience to the Chinamen; they rather seemed to like it, and required no urging to squeeze themselves into tighter compass that they might make room for the little gambling tables, on which dice, dominoes, and fantan helped to keep their little stock of cash in circulation.

There was room enough to gamble, but not room enough for the inevitable gambling fight—if "fight" it may be called; for when an altercation arises among Chinese gamesters, though there is always a good deal of violent gesticulation and a good deal of noise, it is seldom

that any injury is done except to the vocal chords of the
disputants. But such innocent termination of a Chinese
quarrel implies plenty of room for the free play of the
muscles, and this, unfortunately, could not be obtained
on our crowded deck. When the aggrieved gambler, in
Chinese fashion, raised his fist over his shoulder to give
emphasis to some awful imprecation, of necessity he thrust
his elbow against the nose or into the eye of some
innocent observer in his rear. As the man thus unex-
pectedly assaulted raised his fist in the same way, he
inflicted like injury upon someone in the crowd behind
him. Thus every blow threatened or inflicted brought a
new combatant into the fray, until what was at first a
simple dispute between a couple of gamblers became a
general fight. The consequences might have been
disastrous, but at this stage the chief officer adroitly
turned the water-hose upon the battlefield, and, if the
courage of the combatants had been a candle flame, the
cold water could not have more quickly and completely
extinguished it. In a few minutes the gambling tables
were set up again, and the yellow sea of living beings
between the bulwarks of our vessel was, like the blue
sea outside, as peaceful as if it had never been ruffled by
a storm.

But what excitement there was at feeding-time!
Twice a day the Chinese cooks boiled for their fellow-
countrymen three hundred-weight of rice. It was
distributed in wooden buckets—one bucket for ten men;
and, if anything like order had been observed by the

distributors or the recipients, there would have been abundance of food for all. But Chinese stewards would no more think of enforcing discipline than would Chinese coolies of submitting to it, and so, as soon as the rice was ready, there was a wild rush upon the galley. Over every bucket there was a tug of war, dozens of pairs of hands struggling for possession of it. In the tussle many a bucket was upset, and its contents trampled under foot; and so the supply of rice was exhausted long before all had received their share, some of the coolies having to endure an absolutely unbroken fast for several days.

Naturally, the struggle became fiercer as time went on. Standing with the captain on the bridge one morning, and looking down upon that fight for food, it was hard to believe that those engaged in it were human beings. All were stripped to the waist, and, with a babel of confused shouting, they wrestled and fought with one another like beasts of prey.

One sinewy, little man, with eager, hungry look, was struggling vainly in the background. He had not had a morsel of food for a couple of days, and it seemed impossible that he should get any now; but suddenly a thought struck him, and, springing on to the bulwarks of the steamer, he threw himself—not into the water, but into the seething mass of heads and shoulders between him and the cook-house. He literally swam through them to the front, and went down head first among the rice buckets. The first one he touched he seized, and, putting his head inside it, began to eat like a dog. The crowd tried to pull the bucket away from him, but, with one hand on either side, he gripped it like a vice. He was pinched and pommelled, but he would not let go his hold. Even when his feet were lifted from the ground—and men, on the top of the galley, seizing them began to haul the gormand up—for a space the bucket went up with him, and, though his face was hidden, I could see, by the working of the muscles of his neck, that he was still bolting great gulps of rice as fast as he could swallow.

The bucket was torn from the man's grasp at length, and he was flung into the rear. But he seemed little the worse for the conflict. He had received a drubbing, but had been compensated for it by a hearty meal, and, as he rubbed his lips with the back of his hand, his eyes twinkled, and his face beamed with the familiar Mongolian smile—"a smile that was pensive and bland."

But twelve days of this kind of diversion was enough, and hence the joy with which I heard the captain say, on that raw April morning, that Vladivostock was in sight.

CHAPTER II

THE EASTERN TERMINUS

THERE is something forbidding in the aspect of the wild mountain ranges which rise sheer up from the sea to the height of 3000 feet or more along the eastern coast of Siberia; but near the Manchurian frontier, where the Suifoon River finds its way into the sea, there is a break in the range, and the mountains on either side fall away into a group of gently-sloping, round-topped hills. Over the lower slopes of these hills, in the summer-time green with grass and foliage, and over the narrow space between them and the shore, is spread the town of Vladivostock, the eastern terminus of the longest post-road in the world, and of the prospective Trans-Siberian railway.

This town has sprung into existence within the last thirty years, but it is already a well-established settlement, with a population of twenty thousand, half of whom are Europeans. It has not yet attracted much attention in Western Europe, but is regarded by Russia as of great strategic importance, and is likely to become, if it is not already, the most powerful military post in the Far East.

VLADIVOSTOCK.

Opposite the town lies an island several miles in length, and the strait included between it and the mainland forms the harbour—an unusually fine one, deep enough to admit the biggest ship afloat, capacious enough to accommodate the largest fleet, and in all weathers affording safe anchorage.

The general appearance of Vladivostock is very different from that of any other settlement in this part of the world. It seems at first more European, for one is struck at once by the prominence of certain red brick buildings—barracks, I was told they were, but in size and obtrusive ugliness they reminded one of some newly-built cotton-mill in Lancashire. A few of the business houses and residences are also built of red brick; but buildings of this kind are rare, and appear as blots upon the prevailing whiteness of the cosy wooden dwellings, which compose by far the greater part of the town. Most of the houses are detached, and, except in the business quarter, stand in gardens. In these gardens there are plenty of trees — oak, lime, maple, walnut, and such fruit-trees as the apple, pear, and cherry. When these are in full leaf and blossom, Vladivostock, looking down upon the sea from the verdure-covered hillside, is no doubt quite as beautiful as people say; but it seemed dreary enough when I saw it at the end of winter, for the keen frosts had destroyed the foliage and withered up the grass, and there was nothing to be seen but houses and leafless trees.

For nearly six months every year the harbour itself is frozen, and our steamer was one of the first that season to effect an entrance. The few steamers that had got in before us had the paint scraped from their sides by the pack through which they had forced their way; and when we ourselves arrived, the sea to the northward of the harbour was one mass of broken ice as far as the eye could see.

Though in some respects a characteristically Russian town, Vladivostock is very cosmopolitan in its inhabitants. The boatmen who took me ashore, and the porters who carried my luggage to the hotel, were, like most of the day-labourers of the town, Coreans. Many of the smaller shops are kept by Chinamen—from Canton, of course, the most distant but most enterprising portion of the Empire; and very delighted these Cantonese were to meet with a white-faced European who could converse in their own patois. Other shops are kept by Japanese, but these are few.

The principal merchants here are Germans. In the early days of the port two German sailors ran away from their ship here, and opened a little store. That store has developed into the leading mercantile and banking firm in Eastern Siberia; it employs in its house here upwards of fifty European clerks, and has branches in many of the interior towns. There is not a single British merchant at this port, and never will be if the German settlers can have their way; they are angry at the very thought of British competition, and are determined to keep the field they have exploited to themselves.

Russians are, of course, more numerous than other

European residents, but, except the drosky drivers and a few merchants and hotel-keepers, almost all are in Government employ. The military element predominates. The finest plot of land in the neighbourhood is the parade ground; the biggest buildings are the barracks; men in uniform are met with at every turn; and the bray of trumpets and the roll of drums are sounds too familiar to be noticed. The town has also a well-equipped arsenal, a capacious floating dry-dock, and a fleet of torpedo-boats; men-of-war are lying at anchor in the harbour; the heights above the town, though looking innocent enough, are all supposed to have their masked batteries; and it seems to be the ambition of the Czar to make this port a sort of Siberian Sebastopol.

The ice-bound winter, which was just over when I arrived, must have been a lonely time for the European population—cut off from all the world by the frozen sea in front of them, and the 5000 miles of snow behind. But the winter here is far from an unmixed evil, and to the military authorities and the police it is a veritable boon. In the summer they must be always on the warpath. Regarding every stranger as a spy or a rebel, or a villain of some sort, unless he can prove that he is not, their suspicions keep them continually on the alert. If no stranger is in sight, a sharp lookout must be maintained for those who may be coming, and, as if all the world had its eye upon Vladivostock, its brave defenders stand with finger on trigger ready for the fray.

Such vigilance must be very exhausting, and, after

the nervous strain of five or six months of it, the relaxation brought by winter must be an unspeakable relief. No hostile fleet can break through those barriers of ice, and no hostile army can reach them through that wilderness of snow. Even the merchant, however reluctantly, must take a holiday, as free from all shipping worries as if he lived in an inland town. But the whole community responds to the reaction, and the winter season is an unbroken succession of festivities.

At the time of my landing there, Vladivostock was just waking up again to a sense of its responsibilities. The ice has broken up, and who knows what may happen? The merchant is on the lookout for a fresh cargo of provisions from Odessa. The fighting men must again mount guard against the enemy. The police are particularly busy, for steamers are coming in from Japan, and Corea, and China; and aliens are appearing in the streets, whose passports must be examined, and whose movements must be watched, lest, prowling about the town, they should get to know something of the nature and position of its defences.

A fellow-countryman, who had come up from one of the China treaty ports for a holiday, was walking, on the day of his arrival, along the main street of the town, and, because he had a photographic camera in his possession, the police at once arrested him, marched him back to the steamer which brought him, and told him that if he set foot on shore again he would be provided with accommodation which would limit his movements more effectively.

The example of this unfortunate photographer was a warning to me, and I did my very best to escape his fate. I tried to appear uninterested, to be content with furtive glances at the things about me, to have a vacant, expressionless countenance, and, as far as possible, to look like innocence itself.

But all this circumspectness did not save me from suspicion; and when the superintendent of police came to see my passport, he said, in a most searching tone, "On your way from Canton to London? then what brings you here?"

"You have no commission from the British Government?"

"And are not sent out by any English newspaper?"

"Have no other motive than a desire to see the country?"

Then he ceased questioning, and sank into a profound reverie. I could see plainly that he was trying to determine between the two alternatives: was the individual before him a liar or a fool?

CHAPTER III

THE GREAT POST-ROAD

FOLLOWING one of the main streets of Vladivostock to the top of the low range of hills it crosses on the outskirts of the town, the street is seen to be continuous with a road which stretches on before us, until it becomes in the distance a mere brown streak upon the hillside, and then is lost in the forest. That brown streak, running like a thread right through the country and over the Ural Mountains into Europe, is the great post-road which, mainly for military purposes, the Russian Government has constructed across Siberia.

It is a wonderful achievement. Even the Romans, renowned road-makers as they were, never attempted a task of the kind so formidable. Rough enough in many places, and in others little more than a beaten track across the steppe; but it is a marvel to find any practicable way at all across a country not only so unsettled, but so immense.

"If 'Britannia rules the waves,'" once said a Russian officer to me, "remember that Russia rules the land"; and when I stood shivering on the shore at Vladivostock, and thought of the vast expanse of country between me and Europe, I felt as I had never done before the force of that remark. Extending westward from the Pacific Ocean to the Ural Mountains, and northward from the Chinese frontier to the Polar seas, Siberia covers an area of six millions of square miles, is at least a hundred times as large as England, and forms with European Russia the widest continuous stretch of empire in the world.

And the country is as wild as it is extensive. The uniformity of configuration which popular opinion attributes to Siberia is true only of the extreme north, where, along the shores of the Arctic Ocean for a distance of 4000 miles, and inland for a distance of from 150 to 400, lies a dreary waste of treeless and swampy lowland, known to Russians as the Tundra, and which is one immense unbroken plain. The general misconception of Siberia may have arisen from the fact that the earlier Russian settlers in this region made their way eastward across this plain. They did so to avoid the forests and the mountains which made the southern route so difficult, and, still more, to escape the numerous tribes of aborigines, who savagely resisted intrusion into their domains.

But this course across the swamp was practicable only in the winter: it was impossible to establish settlements along the way, and the part of the Pacific coast to which it led was far away from those districts of Eastern Siberia most suitable for agriculture and for pasturage. So at length this northern route to the Pacific was abandoned for one farther south. Adventurous freebooting Cossacks attended to the aborigines, and the engineers set themselves to make the road.

They had no easy task, especially in the eastern half of the country, which is crossed near its centre by the Great Plateau—that immense swelling of the earth's surface which, from the foothills of the Himalayas, extends in a north-easterly direction through Central and Northern Asia to the Behring Straits. This vast table-land tapers towards the north; but in Southern Siberia, where the post-road crosses, it is nearly 1000 miles in breadth, and attains an elevation of 3500 feet above the level of the sea. It is buttressed on either side by mountains which rise to a higher level than itself, forming a sort of cyclopean battlement, and making the plain in this direction inaccessible but for the fact that, like all other battlements, it has its notches—great gaps in the mountain wall through which the ancient glaciers passed to score a winding passage for themselves down to the sea below. Through one of these great natural furrows, which seem like long circuitous valleys between ranges of rugged hills, the post-road finds its way on to the table-land.

But this eastern plateau of Siberia is by no means a continuous plain, for ridges of low hills, following generally a north-easterly direction, break through it here and there, and from its centre rises a second loftier table-land, also walled on either side by mountains, some of whose peaks attain the height of 8500 feet.

East and west of the Great Plateau the road passes through alpine ranges covering an extensive area. Filling many of the valleys of these regions, and spreading far over the table-lands, are immense forests of birch, and larch, and cedar, through which, step by step, the makers of the road have had to cleave their way.

Outside these chains of mountains are other heights and other table-lands, including the western steppes, which, with occasional breaks for the passage of great rivers, extend as far as the Ural Mountains.

The construction of such a length of road was made more difficult and dangerous by the rigour of the climate. The name Siberia has become almost synonymous with wintry cold and desolation, and in this respect the popular opinion is correct. Though it has in most parts a warm, bright summer, beautiful with flowers, and musical with birds and insects, its winters are long and extremely cold. There is not a river or lake in Siberia, nor a harbour on its shores, which is not frozen for about six months in the year. In the northern districts the frost never disappears, for the thaw of the short summer only affects a shallow surface of the soil; and in some of the largest settlements on the Lena the people use ice instead of glass for their window-panes.

If there had been a considerable European population the climatic difficulties would not have been so serious; but the road was carried through extensive tracts of country which, but for a few nomadic Tartars, were absolutely uninhabited, and the workmen had to depend upon themselves for shelter and supplies. The number of settlers in the country has greatly increased since the road was made, but even now the total population of Siberia is not equal to that of London.

Such, then, is the region crossed by the great post-road —an immense expanse of thinly-populated country, in some parts sinking into swamps, in others rising into lofty mountain ranges, and then again spreading itself out in almost interminable plains;—stretches of gloomy forest, and then of treeless waste, with great lakes, wild torrents, and here and there some mighty river rolling northward to the Polar seas.

In a few years more, as the swarm of Chinese navvies on the steamer told me, trains will be running through Siberia. But, at the time now referred to, the short line which runs across the Ural Mountains into Europe was the only railway in the country. Steamers were plying on some of the Siberian rivers, and at certain seasons a considerable part of the journey across the country can be accomplished in this way; but from the coast to the first navigable river, and between one navigable river and another, lay an extensive tract of country, which could only be traversed on the post-road, and where one's only choice was whether he would walk or ride.

Soldiers, poor emigrants, and non-political exiles have to walk, and they spend from six to nine months upon the way. Travellers who can afford to pay for them use horses and a kind of rough phaeton—a springless, four-wheeled carriage, half covered by a hood, and called by the Russians a *tarantass*.

Except in a few settled districts, we depend for our

supply of these conveyances upon the Russian Government, which, for military purposes, has placed a cordon of post-horse stations, from sixteen to twenty miles apart, on all the Siberian roads. A few *yemschiks*—as the post-horse stablemen are called,—and in most cases their wives with them, are put in charge of the station, which is often situated in such a lonely region that these yemschik-households are the sole inhabitants. At these stations officials travelling on urgent business expect to find vehicles and teams of horses ready for them on the shortest notice, and the communications between one military post and another are thus maintained in great efficiency.

Civilians who wish to travel in this way must apply at one of the Government centres for a *podorojna*—a written certificate of permission to use any post-horses which are at liberty, hiring them from one station to the next at a certain charge per horse per mile. The amount is fixed by Government, and a printed table of the charges is posted up on the walls of the travellers' room at every horse-station.

In Vladivostock I obtained a *podorojna*, and, except when steamers were available, travelled on the post-road with horses and tarantass.

CHAPTER IV

THE START

THE worst thing about a cold bath in winter is the first plunge, and in a journey across Siberia there is nothing more trying than the contemplation of the start.

It is better to commence such a journey on the western side, for in this way we reach the wilds by imperceptible degrees, and, what is a still greater advantage, we can start without attracting the attention of our neighbours. The European population of the Far East is small; everybody knows everybody and everybody's movements; and as Siberia is generally regarded as a dreadful country, the man who thinks of crossing it may expect to receive such comments from his compatriots as will not be conducive to his equipment for the journey.

A European resident in China, who attempted to cross Siberia a few years ago, has thus described, with not less truth than simplicity, some of his initial experiences.

"I knew that a journey across Siberia, without a companion, and with barely sufficient funds to secure native means of travel and accommodation, was not a task to be lightly undertaken; but if I had been rash enough to start without sufficient consideration, I met with so many Job's comforters between Hongkong and Vladivostock that I could not fail, before I got there, to be fairly well acquainted with the risks and hardships of the journey.

"'Good-bye,' said one of my friends, 'I never expect to hear of you again.'

"One told me that I should catch my death of cold; another that I should be arrested as a spy, and perish miserably in a Siberian prison.

"Some said it was most likely that I should get lost, and die of starvation in the depths of the forest; others feared that I should be drowned in crossing some of the great rivers; or that I should fall over a precipice; or be devoured by wolves; or kicked to death by wild horses; or murdered by escaped exiles, or some of the wild tribes of the country."

Gloomy as were these premonitions, the traveller declared that they would not have affected him at all "had they not taken a mean advantage—as such evil omens will—of an hour of physical depression due to an attack of ague."

This reference to an ague fit is suspicious. Fevers of this kind are rare in Vladivostock; and were it not for the writer's definite assurance to the contrary, the word in this connection could only be read as a synonym for funk.

The narrative proceeds: "That fit of ague, a parting buffet from the malarious climate I had left, happened to strike me on a typical Siberian winter's day—a day dismal enough to make the blithest spirit pessimistic. A cold, raw, searching wind was blowing; banks of fog were drifting before it; the sky was overcast; and before me in the bay were fields of ice. Chilled to the very bones, and unable to get warm any way, I went to bed. Then it was that those miserable forebodings, which hitherto had kept at a respectful distance, came buzzing in my brain,— 'devoured by wolves,' 'lost in the forest,' 'murdered by brigands.'

"The fog was still drifting past the window; I could hear the wind whistling through the leafless trees; and then, on the table, I caught sight of a portrait which I had been foolish enough to place there, and that made me think of happier scenes. The voice which seemed to whisper in my ear, 'It is not too late, come back!' was only fancy; but it spoke the truth. It was not too late; the steamer which had brought me was still at anchor in the harbour; to-morrow I could re-embark; and this, at length, I resolved to do — I would return to Hongkong and take a passage to Marseilles on a comfortable steamer in the usual way. This resolution was such a soothing one, I fell asleep.

"When I woke next morning the fever had gone, and with it the bad weather. The sun was shining brightly through the window; he had swept the fog from the street and the clouds from the sky, and he swept away the mists from my spirit too. I could laugh at the croaking ravens now, and, lest I should be again tempted to take them seriously, determined to start off at once. So, procuring at the market a 6-lb. loaf and other provisions for the journey, in a few hours Vladivostock, with its steamers, was behind me, and, as fast as three Russian post-horses could go, I was making my way to the Siberian wilds."

This is, in some respects, a representative experience; and few, except Russians, attempt to cross the country from this side without hearing plenty of these gloomy admonitions. It is not merely those who know nothing of Siberia who offer them. A Russian consul, who had once performed this journey, told me that nothing in the world could induce him to attempt it again, and he did his best to persuade me to turn back. Such turning back is not infrequent. Quite recently a party of French residents in China, who had set out for Europe by this route, after a three or four days' journey gave it up, and came back to the coast in a woeful plight.

The present Czar of Russia returned by the Siberian post-road to St. Petersburg after his visit to China and Japan; but all the resources of the country were at his disposal, and such luxurious accommodation and entertainment were provided for him at every stage, that the journey was one long pleasure trip.

Ordinary travellers who need not hurry, and who have funds enough at their disposal to provide their own conveyance and take a servant with them, together with a good supply of provisions, cooking utensils, and bedding, may escape the most serious hardships of such wayfaring; but those who have been accustomed always to the comforts of Western life and modes of travel, and who attempt to cross Siberia in the usual way, must expect to find the journey rough and wearisome in the extreme.

There are no great dangers to be feared. Except a few special ones connected with the wild and unsettled state of the country, the risks of Siberian travel are simply those of a ten miles' drive along any country road, multiplied by a few hundreds to represent the longer distance.

It is these appalling distances which make the prospect of a journey across Siberia so portentous, and the actual experience of it so fatiguing. From one town to the next is sometimes as far as the whole length of England; and, when I thought I had covered at least half the ground between the Pacific Ocean and the Urals, I saw inscribed on the Government notice-board at a post-station —"To St. Petersburg, 5000 miles."

It is not the demands upon one's strength or patience made by any one day's journey, but the unintermitting succession of them from week to week, and month to month, which makes this travel so exhausting; and, unless one has the means of carrying a good supply of provisions with him, he must be content with the simplest fare. After leaving Vladivostock there is no hotel of any kind within a thousand miles. Except when on a steamer, I did not get meat at more than half a dozen places between the Pacific coast and Europe. Milk and eggs and bread and tea make a fairly nutritious dietary; but, after a few months of such a menu, a little variety appears desirable.

But it is not the diet only which is monotonous. There is a monotony of everything. Siberian scenery, as we have already shown, is varied by river, forest, mountain, plain; but of everything there is too much. The rivers are so long, the plains so wide, the forests so vast, and the mountain ranges cover such an extensive area, that one tires of each by turns.

It is no wonder that some of those who commence this journey soon give it up. Except they have been accustomed to the hardships of Siberian life, no women or children, nor anyone not in robust health, should be subjected to it. But if you are a seasoned traveller, not depressed by solitude, tough as leather, patient as a mule, not at all fastidious about what you eat or drink, nor about the condition of your skin and clothing, nor about where you sleep at night,—whether in bed, or on the floor, or in a jolting cart,—if you are such a traveller, you may cross Siberia as the Russians cross it, and quite as much enjoy the journey.

CHAPTER V

FROM THE COAST TO LAKE KHANKA, BY TARANTASS

OUTSIDE Vladivostock we are in the wilds, for there are no suburbs, and, as we lose sight of the buildings of the town, the primeval forest at once comes into view. A broad avenue has been cut through it, and this is our road. We cannot see far before us, for this forest-covered land has been tossed into big, billowy undulations, and our way winds among them. Turning to the right or left, hour after hour, reveals but an endless variety of the same woodland scenes; but at length we emerge into the open, and from the summit of a treeless knoll have a distant view of the white ice-fields of the sea; then again we dip down into the forest, and between "palisades of pine-trees" go on and on, until after a run of twenty miles we come suddenly upon a clearing, and our tired horses are pulled up at the post-station, which terminates the first stage of our journey.

I had looked forward to my arrival at this first post-station with some misgiving, for the yemschiks are reputed to be arrant cheats, and I had been assured in Vladivo-

stock that my ignorance of the country would place me
entirely at their mercy, and that, unless I had allowed a
considerable margin for this cheating, my funds would be
exhausted before I had completed half my journey. As
I had allowed no such margin, there was some reason for
misgiving.

A POST-HOUSE STATION.

The usual method of extortion practised by the yemschiks is to tell the traveller that no Government horses
are available; that the half-dozen or more seen in the
stables are bespoken, or have just returned from a journey,
and cannot, of course, go out again until they have had
their prescribed eight hours' rest; and then obligingly

to offer a private team of their own at an exorbitant charge.

The yemschik here did not think that any subterfuge was needed for imposing upon me, and I had myself inadvertently helped him to this opinion. My knowledge of the language of the people, though sufficient for all the requirements of the journey, was very imperfect, and, to avoid unintelligible questioning, I thought it well to inform the yemschik, after ordering a change of horses, that I did not understand Russian. By the sinister smile upon his face, I saw at once the mistake I had made. These Siberian peasants know nothing of any language but their own, and its importance is, in their judgment, not only relative but absolute; so that for an Englishman to learn English, or a Frenchman French, without learning Russian at the same time, is to them an evidence of quite phenomenal stupidity.

"Does not understand Russian!" I heard the yemschik repeat, with a chuckle to himself.

He repeated it again while sitting at the table to write my bill, and, as he was just then scratching his head over what ought not to have been a very puzzling calculation, I think he must have been trying to decide how much beyond the tariff charges he might prudently extort.

He evidently put some restraint upon his cupidity, for he only added about 50 per cent. to the legitimate charge, and, as the excess amounted to less than two roubles, I would gladly have paid it to avoid delay had I not known that doing so would expose me to similar exactions at the hundred and more post-stations ahead of me, and thus increase my expenditure by many pounds. So I flatly refused to pay more than the authorised charges posted on the wall before me. The yemschik was quite taken aback at finding that one who did not understand Russian was yet able to read it, and he could hardly have looked more bewildered if he had seen a new-born baby get up and speak; but, as I persisted in my refusal, his surprise gave place to indignation, and he declared that if I would not pay the sum he asked, I should not have the horses. "I must then," said I, "try to make myself as comfortable as I can here."

The post-station was simply a series of wooden huts and sheds and stables, around a large quadrangular yard, the whole being enclosed within a strong pine-log stockade. One of the huts at every post-station is reserved for the use of travellers; and this hut is not merely the best but often the only shelter of any kind obtainable throughout a journey of many hundred miles. It measures about twenty feet long by about fourteen wide, and is usually divided by a partition into two apartments. The inside arrangements are of the simplest kind. Its walls and floors are of plain deal, and so is its furniture, which consists of a table, a few chairs, and a bench about two feet wide.

In such a room I established myself to try the issue with the yemschik. The day advanced, and darkness at length came on, but the man showed no sign of yielding, so I spread my blankets on the floor and went to sleep. In the middle of the night I woke at the sound of someone in the room, and saw a man with a lantern moving towards me. It was only the yemschik; and when I asked him what he wanted, he said, "I will take a rouble less for the horses."

"Not a kopek more than the tariff rate," was my reply, and the man left me again to the darkness and my reflections.

But he was evidently beginning to feel uneasy lest some Russian officer should pass that way—as at any hour he might—and the attempted extortion should get reported at headquarters. The next morning he was most obliging, inquired when I wished to start, had the horses brought out at once, asked for and received the legal hire, and I was soon on my way again.

I had no further difficulty of this kind. At the next station I said nothing about the slenderness of my acquaintance with the Russian language, but simply gave my orders to the yemschik, and they were promptly attended to. Though I had to change the whole turnout—horses, tarantass, and driver—I was off again within twenty minutes from the time of my arrival.

This part of the post-road ran through a lonely and unsettled country. There was no house of any kind, not even a wayside cottage, between one station and another. A wreath of smoke in the distance sometimes led us to expect one, but on coming nearer we found a little company of Russian emigrants or soldiers, who, after a long tramp, had found a convenient resting-place, and, on the ground padded with withered pine-leaves, were lounging round a fire to boil the millet which, with black bread and tea, constitutes their daily food.

To make up for time lost at the first post-station, I pushed on all day from stage to stage as fast as possible. The air was cold and bracing, and there was not at this season anything to tempt one to linger by the way. The frost had only just broken, and the whole country was still in winter dress. The snow had gone from the level ground; but the places where it had gathered in deep drifts, or banked itself up beside the road, were still marked by heaps of ice. All around us was a waste of faded leaves and withered vegetation; and in one place, giving a deeper shadow to the desolation, was a lonely Siberian graveyard. It was only a small enclosure, separated from the wilds by a rough wooden paling, and containing fifty or sixty graves, each marked by a white wooden cross. Except on the fir-trees there were no green leaves to be seen, but the sombre brown of road and forest was not without relief, for the sun was shining over white banks of cloud, and everything which could reflect his radiance—the silver bark of the birch-trees, and the clumps of everlasting daisies which here and there shone out from the surrounding masses of dead leaves like bits of gold—did their best to brighten up the scene; while the catkins hanging from the willow-boughs told us of the coming spring-time, and the white crosses on the graves of the resurrection morning.

After a long spin through this wild scenery and wintry air, one can appreciate the comforts of the travellers' room at the post-station. In summer these wooden shelters swarm with vermin, but from such torment travellers at this season of the year are free. There is no fire-grate to be seen, but a big brick bread-oven, whose mouth opens outside on to the stableyard, projects into one corner of the room. Whether the yemschiks are baking bread or not, Imperial order directs that plenty of good logs shall be burnt in this oven every day, and so, however intense the cold outside, the travellers' room is always comfortably warm. In Siberia this is not so much a luxury as a necessity, for it would be impossible to cross these extensive tracts of country in the winter-time without the opportunity of thawing oneself now and then upon the way. There are no provisions to be had at any of these stations except milk and eggs and coarse black bread, but there is always ready for the traveller at five minutes notice a *samovar* of boiling water. A samovar is simply a large brass urn with a hollow cylinder running up through the middle of it to contain burning charcoal, and thus to keep the water boiling as long as required. With the samovar the yemschik brings a small teapot and a glass goblet; the traveller himself must provide the tea and sugar.

The sissing of the samovar sounded specially cheerful to me that night after my first long day's journey. We did not arrive at the station until an hour after sunset, but had covered that day a distance of over a hundred miles, and I had not tasted food since early morning. In such circumstances, eggs and milk, with the tea and bread and tinned butter brought with me from the coast, were enough for a hearty meal; one craved no other luxuries.

Travellers in Siberia do not usually limit their travelling to the daytime. They get what sleep they require in the tarantass, and never stop except to change their horses until they reach their journey's end. But, not being yet accustomed to this mode of travel, one long day of it was sufficiently fatiguing, and as the travellers' room at this station seemed so snug and quiet I resolved to stay here till morning. It was a lonely spot, no other house within many miles, and the forest closed round the station on every side. The yemschiks and their families were in the neighbouring log-huts, and I had the travellers' hut to myself. On the previous night, not knowing what might happen, I had slept in my clothes, but all seemed so private and secluded here that I thought I might venture to sleep in the ordinary way. So, having arranged my rugs and blankets on the wooden bench, I undressed, turned the lamp low, and lay down for a long night's rest.

I suppose I had been asleep for several hours, when the tramp of horses woke me, and a minute afterwards a yemschik entered the room to turn up the lamp, and in came a company of travellers—four gentlemen and two ladies. To have one's sleep disturbed and one's bedroom invaded in this unceremonious fashion was more than I was prepared for; but when I caught sight of the ladies I was horrified to think of my deshabille, and I had barely time to snatch my garments from the chair on which I had placed them, when one of the ladies advanced to take possession of it. I bundled my clothes under the blankets as quickly as I could, and then made desperate efforts to put them on; but anyone who has ever tried, as an experiment, to dress himself beneath heavy blankets and a big fur rug on a rickety bench scarcely eighteen inches wide, will understand how impossible it is. I was once within a hair's-breadth of a dreadful catastrophe, for, had not a heavy person been sitting on the chair I suddenly gripped to restore my lost equilibrium, the bench would have turned over and rolled me into the middle of the room.

I was not rash enough to disregard this warning, and, lest something worse should happen, I resolved to lie as still as possible until the people were asleep. I had not to wait long. The travellers had evidently had a weary journey, perhaps of many days, and after a hasty supper each selected a place upon the floor for rugs and blankets, and in a few minutes I was the only one in the room awake. And there was no mistake about it, for the sleeping was not only audible but loud. The room was a small one, and I doubt whether the same number of accomplished snorers have ever been assembled at once in a space so limited before. It was awful. The cacophony was by no means uniform, and I could easily distinguish at least five distinct varieties of snoring. One was in high-pitched key like the subdued mewing of a cat, another like distant moaning of the wind, another like the squeaking of an unoiled pump, another like the growling of a dog, and yet another like the snorting of a horse. When the concert was in full swing I got up to dress, the noise assuring me that I might take my time about it. I never knew before that discord could be so composing.

Being dressed, I felt like a different being. The craven, shrinking, coward spirit which I had before gave place at once to one of independence and defiance. I began to feel indignant with the sleepers for making such a noise,—for the snoring, having served its purpose, was no longer interesting, and threatened to keep one awake all night; but, like all other noises, one can get accustomed to it, and at length in spite of it I slept in peace.

When I woke next morning the other travellers were sleeping still, and I had to stride over them to get out of the room. The yemschiks also, though moving about in the stables, were hardly yet awake, and took nearly an hour to get my horses yoked. When at last all was ready, and I was about to step into the conveyance which I had waited for so patiently, another tarantass came dashing down the road, and was pulled up at the station. Its occupant was a Russian officer, who no sooner alighted from his own conveyance than, with a word to the yemschik, he sprang into mine and at once drove off. This is one of the commonest vexations of civilian travellers on the Siberian post-road, but they cannot reasonably complain. "The king's business required haste." The road, the supply of horses, and the line of post-stations have all been established by the Government for its own purposes. It is only by courtesy that other travellers have permission to use them, and they receive that permission on the distinct understanding that if Government officers require their horses they will deliver them up at once.

Another tarantass is soon brought out, and while the horses are being yoked we have time to observe the characteristics of this strange-looking type of vehicle. A tarantass is neither a trap, nor a buggy, nor a cart, nor a waggon, but a sort of conveyance which combines the inconveniences of all. I suppose it is specially adapted for Siberian post-road service, and, in the language of the naturalists, owes its peculiarities of structure to the exigencies of its environment.

There are two pairs of wheels, whose axles are fixed under the extremities of a couple of parallel poles made of some tough kind of timber, and measuring from 10 to 15 feet in length, according to the distance between the fore and aft pair of wheels; these poles compensate to some extent for the absence of metal springs, which would be smashed to pieces in the first wild gallop on these rough roads. Resting upon the parallel poles is the cradle-shaped body of the vehicle, from six to eight feet in length and about five feet wide, and in most cases made of sheet-iron supported by a frame of wood. This frame is extended upward at the back and sides, so as to form over the hinder half a sort of hood, which is made water-tight by an outside covering of leather. There is a box in front for the driver, but there is no other seat of any kind. The passenger's luggage is carefully arranged at the bottom of the conveyance, a layer of straw is spread over it, and the passenger himself must keep things in position by sitting or reclining on the top.

The tarantass is usually drawn by a team of three horses. The steadiest and strongest animal is put in the

OUR TARANTASS.

shafts, each of which is loosely hooked on to the vehicle, but is united to its fellow shaft in front by a wooden yoke of horseshoe shape, which arches over the horse's neck. To the top of this yoke is attached the bearing rein, and from it are suspended two or three bells, which jingle in time to the horse's trot, and perhaps help to drive off the wolves. The other two horses to the right and left of the central one are attached by strong rope traces to the projecting ends of the fore axle-tree. Thus yoked, the three horses strikingly remind us of the teams we have seen in pictures of the chariot races of ancient Rome.

Having arranged our baggage in the tarantass, and placed ourselves upon the top, we are ready to start. The horses are of medium size, rough-haired, raw-boned, and altogether sorry-looking beasts; but their looks are the worst part of them, for they have not only plenty of "go" in them, but plenty of staying power as well, and, often after a most despondent contemplation of the team provided for me, I have found myself travelling at quite unusual speed, and keeping it up from hour to hour.

And now the yemschik, in his sheepskin coat, and with a fur cap upon his head, mounts the box, and off we go. He has, of course, a whip, and the two side horses stand out on either side, at an angle of several degrees from the line of progress, that they may keep their eye upon that whip. But the driver does not use it much; he can do so when required, as the horses evidently know, but on ordinary occasions it is quite enough to raise his hand. He regulates his horses' speed by talking to them; whether or not they understand Russian, he treats them as if they did. While they are going satisfactorily he calls them his "little turtle doves"; as their speed slackens he begins to use terms which are not so complimentary and endearing; and when at length his patience is exhausted he calls them awful names—names so awful, indeed, and uttered with such emphasis, that at the sound of them the horses usually rush off in a fright.

Every Russian traveller in Siberia carries one or two large pillows with him. He may have little other baggage, no box or bag or portmanteau, but he always has his pillows. We are inclined to laugh at him at first, but before one stage of our journey is completed we see that laughter would be more appropriate the other way. The roads of Siberia are as well made and as well preserved as one could reasonably expect in such a thinly-populated region, but they are rough roads at the best. If the course is obstructed by a bit of swampy land or a mud-hole, a few logs are rolled into it, and sometimes a considerable extent of quaggy road is made practicable in this way—by covering it with a tranverse layer of tree-trunks. The tarantass, wherever possible, is always driven at full gallop, and as we go bumping over these tree-trunks we know why travellers acquainted with the country are careful to take pillows with them.

In some parts the road crosses range after range of hills, and there is a long succession of deep declivities and steep ascents. At the bottom of almost every valley runs a small river; and if it is too deep to ford, we find that several tall pines have been thrown across from one bank to the other, a sufficient number of pine-logs have been laid athwart them, and thus is produced that peculiar structure known as a "corduroy bridge."

When we arrive at the brow of the hill overlooking one of these deep valleys, the driver looks not only at the slope before him but at the steep ascent beyond, and his aim is to go down the hill at such a speed that the horses cannot stop themselves until they get well up the acclivity upon the other side. So he leans suddenly forward, spreads out his hands like wings over the horses, shouts at the top of his voice, " Hee! hee!" and away down the steep we go, at such a break-neck pace that when we reach the corduroy bridge at the bottom we strike it with a shock which makes the tarantass leap into the air.

Then we know not only why the Russians always take pillows with them, but why there is a cover at the back of the conveyance. Heretofore we had innocently thought it was intended to screen us from the sunshine and the rain, but we see now that it must be meant also to prevent us from being shot too far into the air, for after going up a certain distance one's head strikes against the woodwork, which sends us down again more quickly even than we went up, and happy are we then if we have some good soft pillows to fall down upon.

How did I like it? Why, at first—to speak guardedly —not much. None of my joints were actually dislocated, though several of them felt as if they were, and for a week or more every bone in my body ached. Many a time I regretted that I had not brought more pillows with me. But the instinct of self-preservation led me at length to discover the position of most stable equilibrium; and I learned so to adjust myself — holding on to ropes and straps, with one foot pressed firmly against this projection and the other against that—and so to arrange the straw

FAST DRIVING.

and pillows, that after a little time for training I could travel like this all day and all night, and from day to day, and even week to week, without feeling much the worse.

But it was trying to the nerves as well as to the coarser tissues, and my first few days of tarantass-riding were days of great anxiety. Often, as at headlong speed we shot down some deep descent, I thought we should be dashed to pieces; but as this did not happen, I came at length to regard these mad gallops with indifference, and at last with reckless enjoyment. The spirit of the Russian driver so infected me that we never seemed to go too fast. I could feel the exhilarating influence of the wild rushing of the steeds; and often, as we prepared for a daring dash down some precipitous hillside, when the yemschik shouted "Hee! Hee!" the horses heard a second voice repeating it.

Our tarantass experiences in this part of the journey were not always so exciting. About a hundred and fifty miles to the north of Vladivostock the post-road dips down from the hill-country, and half loses itself in a swampy plain. This plain is part of an extensive tract of lowland, which fills up the angle between the right bank of the Usuri and the lower waters of the Amoor. In a comparatively recent geological period it was covered by the sea, and some of the rivers which run through it do not even yet seem quite decided as to the channel in which they ought to flow. Often in the early summer they break out over the plain, inundating hundreds of square miles of country, and making this part of the post-road quite impassable.

We had no fear of floods so early in the year, but the winter is the only season in which this marshy region can be crossed without some apprehension of disaster or delay. For eight hours we had been picking our way through the morass; we ought to have reached the next station in less than half the time, but no station was yet in sight, nor had we, since we started, seen a sign of any human being or human dwelling-place. There was no reliable track for us to follow, and our yemschik made many a long detour in the hope of keeping on solid ground. But in spite of this care and patience our tarantass gave a sudden lurch, and sank up to the axles in a mud-hole. All our efforts to extricate it were in vain. The driver urged the horses until the two side ones broke their traces and scoured away over the plain. The horse in the shafts did his best to follow them, but his hind feet were fast in the slough, and he could only use the one free forefoot to dash mud into my face. I leaped out on to a little patch of dry land—a sort of island in the swamp—and then the driver, having released the horse from the shafts and caught the two others, rode away with them to the next station, six or seven miles distant, to get another vehicle.

We had to wait three hours for his return; and for testing the delights of isolation in a swamp three hours is long enough. A Russian traveller had asked me at a previous station to allow him, for the next stage or two, to share my tarantass, so I had one companion. The day was dull and dreary, and the scenery was like it. We had an uninterrupted view of the horizon and the intervening plain, but there was nothing better to be seen than a few tufts of withered grass and bulrushes.

Our presence in this sequestered spot was slightly suggestive of a picnic, but when I tried to fancy that it was — to make the time pass more pleasantly — my imagination was not equal to the effort. Picnics usually take place in warm summer weather; I was shivering with cold. At a picnic a provision basket is essential, and it was specially essential in this case, for I had not had anything whatever to eat or drink since the preceding day. Picnics are always graced with a few fair specimens of the heavenlier half of our humanity, but the wildest vagaries of fancy could not associate ideas of beauty with this rough, bearded Russian.

No; whatever else our position was, it certainly was not romantic. There was not much to see, and there was still less for us to do. The Russian wished he had a pipe, or at least some tobacco; and I wished I had—it must have been a book; but whichever was the more virtuous wish, both were equally in vain. We could either sit on the cold ground or stand, but if we attempted walking we got into a quagmire. The only exercise available to keep our blood in circulation was shouting, and our only amusement was scanning with a field-glass that point on the horizon where the yemschik had disappeared. Sometimes these two occupations were combined, for our vision was too eager to be true, and the sight of a bird flying low in the distance, or of a reed shaken by the wind, so raised our hopes of rescue that we yelled at one another, "Horses!" "Horses!" "Horses!"—until at length, out of humour with disappointment, and out of breath with exertion, we dropped again into a morose silence. When we had given up looking for them, the horses came; we did not see them until we heard the yemschik's voice, but we were soon on our way again, and at four o'clock in the afternoon we reached the post-station, having left the previous one at about the same hour in the morning. Here I got my breakfast.

After five or six days of this kind of travel I was quite ready for a change, and was not sorry, on crossing the brow of a low range of hills, to see before me in the distance the white surface of Lake Khanka, and to know that the troubles of tarantass-riding were for the present at an end.

CHAPTER VI

LIFE IN A SIBERIAN VILLAGE

THE next two thousand miles of the post-road only exists for six months in the year. On no other part of it is travelling so easy and so expeditious, and yet it cost absolutely nothing in the making, for it is simply the frozen surface of Lake Khanka and of the river system communicating with it.

Except for its unwonted smoothness—the absence of shocks and bangs and joltings—travel on the ice is very similar to that upon the land. At the post-stations on the banks of the river teams of horses are supplied, and the sledge behind them is simply a tarantass provided with runners instead of wheels.

When this part of the post-road has been obliterated by the heat of summer, steamers take the place of sledge and horses, and thus maintain the continuity of route; but at the beginning and end of every winter there is an indefinite period in which neither mode of travel is available, the ice being too abundant for navigation, and too weak and broken for surface traffic.

In such a period—just at the close of the winter

season) too early for a steamer and too late for a sledge—I reached the shores of Khanka Lake. A fortnight before a traveller had crossed upon the ice, but I gathered from his conversation that he had not very much enjoyed the trip. He had set out from the other side with a sledge and three horses at ten o'clock at night, and, as the distance from one bank to the other is about forty miles, it took upwards of four hours to complete the journey. As the ice even then was not considered absolutely safe, an extra fee had been paid to the driver to reconcile him to the risk. The easy motion of the sledge soon lulled the traveller to sleep, and he did not wake until midnight, when he was annoyed to find they were standing still. The yemschik had only stopped to get his pipe and some tobacco for a smoke; but as this is a rather slow and difficult operation for one so encumbered with heavy sheepskins, he tried to divert the attention of the evidently impatient traveller by narrating a few reminiscences. "I recollect," said he, "that just about a year ago, on a pitch-dark night like this, as near as possible to this same hour, and within a yard or two of the very spot where we are now—some twenty miles or so from either shore — the ice suddenly gave way, and a sledge and three horses, with two travellers and a yemschik, went down without a moment's warning to the bottom of the lake."

The traveller did not seem to appreciate this story, or, if he did, he showed his appreciation in a very peculiar way. He called the man a drivelling idiot, and threatened to knock him off the box if he did not instantly shut up his yarning and drive on.

I don't think the traveller slept much during the remainder of the journey. He was an educated man, and was reputed to have some taste in music, but I heard him say that the sweetest sound he ever heard was that of sledge-runners, in the early morning, crunching through the shingle of a beach.

There was evidently no chance for me to continue my journey until the south wind brought a thaw, but the delay was not without its compensation. I had been so shaken, not to say bruised and battered, by the antics of the tarantass, that I could appreciate the benefit of rest; and a week or two in Kamenrubeloff could not fail to give me some interesting information with regard to Siberian village life.

Kamenrubeloff means "fisherman's rock," and there is no doubt a romance connected with the designation, but I only know it as the name of a village on Lake Khanka. It is a dreary little place, and especially so at this season of the year. One could not walk far eastward without coming abruptly to the edge of the cliff-like alluvial bank, which falls precipitously forty or fifty feet to the lake shore; but around the village on all other sides lay an open, undulating country, only partially reclaimed and cultivated. On some of the hillsides were woods of birch and alder, but, except the brown remnants of the previous summer's foliage, there was hardly a leaf or a grass blade to be seen.

Most Siberian villages have only one street, which, however, is broad enough for a market-place; but Kamenrubeloff has a second equally broad street, cutting the first at right angles. The village has no terraces and no two-storied houses, its dwellings, with the exception of the soldiers' quarters in the suburbs, consisting entirely of

LOG-HOUSE.

pine-log cottages, which, with a varying interval between them, are ranged on either side the road. Though small, they are snug and substantial structures. The logs of which they are built are so shaped as to fit closely to the adjacent ones, they are dovetailed into each other at the ends, and support a double roof of thatch and boarding.

With few exceptions the outside timbers are discoloured by age, and the only paint about them is on the window-frames and doors.

Most of the cottages stand back from the road, each one in a small fenced enclosure of its own, within which might be seen some farming implements, a rough Siberian cart, a horse, a cow, a few black pigs, and perhaps some barn-door fowls. Among the houses which stand close upon the street are a few shops for the sale of vodka, groceries, and clothing; but there is nothing to distinguish them from the neighbouring cottages except the wares exposed in their windows.

As there was no hotel in the village, nor a lodging-house of any kind, I had to seek for shelter in one of the private houses. Pushkoff, the Russian land surveyor, who was with me in the swamp, had come to the village, and was also waiting for a steamer, so he proposed that if he could find a room I should share it and its expenses with him. The first place we secured was such a den of misery that even Pushkoff was dissatisfied, but the next day we succeeded in finding more comfortable quarters—a clean little room of about fourteen feet by ten, its walls, ceiling, and floor of smooth unpainted pine, and having two small windows—one looking into the farmyard at the back, and the other looking out upon the road. Its furniture consisted of two chairs, a table, and a broad wooden bench which served me for a bed; the Russian, characteristically, preferred to sleep upon the floor.

He was vexed that I would not consent to share

board as well as lodging with him, but I knew too much already of his household ways. He was a good-natured man, and when I was passing through the village where he lived he invited me to dinner at his house. There were three of us at table—Pushkoff, his wife, and myself; we had each a knife and fork, but there were no plates, and we all three had to help ourselves out of the one dish, which contained a mixture of some kind of minced meat and vegetables. Such an arrangement is convenient; it saves a good deal of dish-washing and other labour, but it has this great disadvantage—it makes it impossible for a slow eater to get his fair share of the feast; so I told Pushkoff that it would be better for each of us to cater for himself.

Soon after he brought in a pickled salmon, which he had purchased from a farmer in the village, and laid it, dripping with brine, upon our only table; there it lay until the Russian had eaten it, which, as the fish weighed over twenty pounds, was not for a considerable time. He had no stated hour for meals, and no stated number of them; but whenever he felt hungry he cut, with a large pocket-knife, a slice out of the salmon and ate it raw, washing it down with a glass or two of tea or vodka.

The table was soon covered from one end to the other with brine and fragments of fish, and the only place where I could have meals in comfort was the window-sill; but during my first few days in Kamenrubeloff the difficulty was to get the meals. Black bread and salt fish seem to be the staple food of these Siberian peasants, and I did

not find either to my taste. The rye-flour, of which the
bread is made, is said to be mixed with powdered pine-
bark, and certainly its taste is pungent enough for
anything; however hungry, a finger's-breadth of it was
sufficient to take away my appetite. I had to have salt
fish, whether I would or not; though I never actually
ate a morsel of it in this village, I feasted my eyes on it
all day, and imbibed its exhalations all night; and if I
ever felt a craving for food I did not possess, I had only
to look at that fish-smeared table, and the pangs of hunger
were allayed. Beef and mutton were only seen among
the villagers on rare occasions, and, as to milk and eggs,
the people told me that the cows were dry, and that the
hens had not yet begun to lay. But by persistent search
I discovered one milch cow at a farm on the outskirts of
the village; by going from house to house I managed to
buy up, one here and another there, a score or so of
eggs; then I met a Chinaman, who sold me a dozen
pounds of rice; and at last I was so well provided for—
in the opinion of these villagers—that I could fare
sumptuously every day.

It is a saying of the Chinese that "Europeans must
be a very dirty people, or they would not find it
necessary to wash so frequently." They would form a
higher opinion of us if they saw us here. There were no
facilities for washing in these cottages, and cold water
for such a purpose is quite out of favour in Siberia. The
peasants sometimes take a vapour bath, or, in the absence
of convenience for this, get into the bread oven when it

has sufficiently cooled down, and, when they have soaked in perspiration long enough, come out and rub themselves briskly with a handful or two of snow. This is expected to keep their skin clean and supple for at least half a year.

At one of the post-stations I ventured to hint that I would like a wash. I was asked to go out into the yard, where I saw a servant standing with a teacup of cold water. Holding out my hands she poured a little of the water over them, I rubbed my hands together and held them out again, when the remaining water in the cup was emptied over them that I might rub it on my face; and this is all the ablution which even the most fastidious consider necessary.

At other post-stations the assistance of the servant is rendered unnecessary by what the people regard as a very ingenious contrivance. A small brass funnel is fixed against the wall, about four feet from the ground. Anyone anxious for a wash has only to pour a teacupful of water into this funnel, and if he is quick enough he may lave his hands and face while the water is trickling through.

Pushkoff told me, the first day I spent with him, that cold tea was better than water for washing purposes; and in the evening I noticed that, when he had drunk all he required, he filled up the teapot again. The next morning, before I had risen from my bench, I saw my companion sitting on the front-door step with the teapot in his hand. He put the spout to his lips, as if to take a deep drink, then replacing the teapot by his side, and making a syringe of his mouth, he held up his hands and spirted the tea out over them; when he had rubbed them sufficiently, he applied more tea in the same way to rub over his face, and his ablution was complete.

There was plenty of tea left in the pot, but I preferred to take my towel to the shore of the lake; the ice had melted along its margin, and its clear cold water was good enough for me; but every splash involved a penalty, and sometimes for nearly an hour after my hands were completely paralysed.

With the exception of a few Chinese, the people of this village were Russians, and typical examples of Siberian peasantry. Some of them were always in sight from the window of my room—the men in blue blouses and top-boots, with their long hair cut evenly all round, and half covered by bearskin caps, were busy preparing their gear for tillage, mending their houses, or fetching cartloads of fuel from the forest; and the women in their short print gowns, bareheaded, and as often as not barefooted, were hurrying about the little farmyards, attending to their poultry and cattle.

The more one knew of these people, the more interesting they became. Beneath their rugged features and coarse manners beat kind and honest hearts; and, dull and slow-witted as they seem, their energy of character reveals itself not only in their power of enduring hardship, but in the dogged determination with which they are subduing this wild country to their service. In contrast with the most refined of the natives of that so-called Celestial

Empire to the south of them, their superiority is striking. In every circumstance of life but their religion, the Chinese seem to have the advantage of them — better climate, more fertile soil, and easier life; but to compare the two is like comparing uncut diamonds with pieces of polished jadestone.

Some of the villagers were exiles whose term of imprisonment had expired, but most of them were free emigrants. Many of the settlers in these remote regions came here to escape oppression, either in the shape of the conscription or of religious persecution. To save themselves from being sent out to Siberia, they came here of their own freewill. The security of such fugitives depended upon the distance to which they wandered, and, as on Russian territory they might at any time be arrested and punished for their flight, they aimed at going beyond the frontier, and forming settlements on alien soil. This district was the home of Russian emigrants before it formed part of the Russian Empire; but in no case did such settlements remain long outside: no sooner did the Government hear of a colony of Russians in a region beyond the frontier, than the frontier was extended to include it. It was as if the boundaries of the empire had been an elastic cord, which clung to the fugitives as they tried to push beyond it, so that whatever spot they selected for their settlement became, because of such selection, Russian soil. The hardy Cossacks, living, eating, sleeping in the saddle, kept the forefeet of their horses on the receding frontier, and if, after the inclusion by it of some extensive tract of country in Manchuria, a Chinese mandarin ventured to suggest that yesterday this boundary stone was a score of miles to the westward of its position now, the Cossack curtly answered, " Well, there the stone is now, and I am here ; what have you to say ? "

Well for him he said nothing, but went quietly away. And so the Czar's dominion, with the steadiness and persistency of an advancing tide, has spread itself over the vast territories of Northern Asia, until it has become conterminous with the Pacific Ocean and the Japan Sea.

The nearest settlement to Kamenrubeloff was many miles away, and there was absolutely no scattered population ; but a company of gipsies happened to have pitched their tents on the outskirts of the village, and had spent the winter there. They were the most respectable and romantic-looking gipsies I have ever seen — altogether different from the ragged, unkempt creatures one meets sometimes in English lanes. By their aristocratic bearing as they strolled about the village, and by the rough courtesy with which the people treated them, it was evident that they were by no means regarded as pariahs either by the villagers or by themselves.

The men wore top-boots, black sheepskin coats, and fur caps ; the chiefs of the tribe being distinguished from the rest by a row of bulb-shaped buttons of chased silver as large as a good-sized apple. The women were fond of red cotton-dresses ; and those of higher rank were made still more conspicuous by a string of forty or fifty silver dollars round the neck. Every morning a number of them passed my window on the way down to the lake for water, which they carried up in bright copper vessels on their head. They were anything but shy, and the visits of these gipsy ladies were most unceremonious and inopportune. They simply opened my door and walked in; and if, as was frequently the case, I happened to be having dinner when they called, they drew up to my window-sill diningtable in a most free and friendly way, and helped themselves to whatever they fancied of my frugal meal.

The gipsy men called once or twice, and kindly tried to dissuade me from venturing farther on this journey by telling me of the dangers and difficulties encountered by themselves in coming here, and of the number of their tribe who had perished on the way.

One of them sometimes came into the village in the evening, and borrowed an accordion, upon which he played a lively polka; and at once, as by a spell, the doors of the log-cottages flew open, and the villagers came out and danced until the darkness and chill air of night sent them all home to bed.

This was not the only music the village could supply. One day, when quietly sitting in my room, I heard a burst of singing which quite startled me, for it was not the careless droning of some peasant sauntering about his farm, but singing by a multitude of voices, and with heart and will. The air was a strange one, but there was plenty of wild stirring music in it, and the time was perfect. I could see nothing of the singers, but the sound of their voices seemed to approach so rapidly I might have thought them a troop of angels bearing down upon the village from the sky, but for the moving cloud of dust which now appeared in the distance, and through which at length I saw the shape of horses and riders and the gleam of polished steel. The cloud came on apace, and in a few moments a company of Cossacks, still singing their wild martial ballad, went sweeping by on their way to some distant station.

British cavalry sometimes relieve, by singing, the monotony of a long journey; but in England we generally associate a vocal chorus out of doors with Salvation Army services or Methodist camp-meetings. Neither the one nor the other are yet known in Siberia, but every important village has its church.

The church is the only public building here. It stands in the middle of the village, and is conspicuous not only by its size but its appearance, for the pine-logs of which it is constructed are painted white, its tower is topped by a pale-green dome, and above all shines a gilded cross. To see the building at a distance, with a cluster of cottages around it, suggests the fancy of some gigantic bird among its fledgelings — a fancy not altogether false, for the relationship between the church and the dwellings which surround it is not one of juxtaposition merely: without it Kamenrubeloff would be but a miscellaneous assemblage of independent homesteads; the presence of a place of worship establishes a bond between them, and gives to the village something of organic unity.

Whatever the moral character of these villagers may

be, they always reverence the church. Whenever they pass by it they doff their hat, and there are few who do not sometimes attend its services. For those who have to mind the house on Sunday mornings, to allow the other members of the family to go to church, a special service is held every Saturday night. Pushkoff, my companion, responded promptly to the call of church bells, and when he attended service I generally went with him.

Compared with its exterior of spotless white, the inside of the church looked gloomy, its dark pine-wood walls being left unpainted; but the lower part was relieved by numerous pictures and images of saints, and there was no lack of paint and gilding on the reredos and altar, which in Russian churches generally are even more ornate than those of the Church of Rome. A seller of candles stood in the porch; and all who came to church, except the very poor, were expected to purchase one. It was passed by a verger to the front, where it was lit and fixed in one of the numerous candle-holders near the altar; the brilliancy of the illumination being supposed to represent the size and devoutness of the congregation.

There are no seats in the building, so that worshippers must either stand or kneel. The service was intoned throughout, the clerk giving the responses in deep bass. There was no sermon, and it is very seldom that there is one in any of these Russian churches. The universal surveillance of the Government, and the ease with which an innocent expression may be construed into heterodoxy or high treason, make preaching too risky; and as sermons are not prescribed parts of the service, it is the safest course to omit them altogether.

At the end of the service every Sunday morning the Sacrament of the Lord's Supper was administered to a number of recently-baptized infants. Adults think it sufficient for themselves to partake of the ordinance once or twice a year, but it is considered advisable for baptized babies to do so every Sunday until they are twelve months old. In all Russian churches the bread and wine are mixed together, and the mixture is administered, both to children and adults, in a silver spoon. A dozen infants were carried by their mothers to the altar; each in turn had a silken bib arranged under its chin by the priest; and then, while the choir chanted, the frightened children, some of whom screamed outright, received, much against their will, the sacred elements.

After the conclusion of the service, the priest—or pope, as the Russians call him—stood in front of the altar, holding out a large silver cross. The entire congregation filed forward to the front to kiss this cross before they left the church.

It was rather surprising to find that a church so ritualistic sometimes held out-door services; but I happened to be in this village on St. George's day. While having breakfast in the early morning I heard the tramp of many feet, and, going to the door, saw the priest in his robes of office at the head of a procession, following the banner of St. George. At the crossways in the centre of the village the procession halted, and soon I saw, drawing towards it from every side, the strangest crowd I ever heard of in connection with church services.

St. George is regarded as the patron saint of domestic animals, and it is believed that some special blessing will rest upon the cattle if once a year, on this saint's feast-day, they join in public worship. And so they were now on their way to the service—flocks of sheep, with herds of cattle, swine, and horses, making when they came together a most motley congregation. But the poor beasts were not religiously inclined, or did not appreciate this kind of worship, and it took half the bipeds of the congregation to keep the quadrupeds from bolting, one or two of the pigs being so depraved that they knocked their benefactors over and ran away. But when at length the service opened, and the congregation began to sing, what with the bleating of the sheep, the neighing of the horses, the bellowing of the cattle, the squealing of the pigs, and the barking of a score or two of irreverent dogs who would neither join the circle of the worshippers nor go away, but stood around protesting loudly while priest and people did their best to make their voices heard above the others, the combination made a chorus the like of which, even in Bedlam, you might listen for in vain.

The social life of a little community of peasants, in such a remote corner of the earth, might seem to an outsider dull. But the people themselves are not conscious of this dulness; they know nothing better than their village life, and are content. They never see a newspaper, and except by an occasional letter from their friends, or the arrival of some passing traveller, have no means of knowing what is happening in other portions of the world; but this only makes them take a deeper interest in local circumstances, and in one another's family affairs. With so much in their own circle to awaken interest—births and deaths; betrothals and marriages: the fortunes of the battle in which they are engaged with nature; the varying aspects of sky and lake and forest, from season to season, and even from day to day; the play and interplay of human passions and affections, with their multiform developments, tragic, pathetic, or amusing: and the frequently recurring services at church, with the glimpses they get there of the infinite and the eternal,— with all this, these simple villagers cannot understand why we should consider their position lonely or their life monotonous, and they never think with anything like envy of the residents in busy towns.

A day or two after St. George's festival I noticed that something unusual was astir, and presently one of the villagers asked me if I was not going to see the wedding. No one whose human sympathies are not completely petrified can fail to feel some thrill of pensive interest in a wedding, though the bridal pair are utter strangers and of the humblest class; but a Siberian wedding had for me the added charm of novelty, and I hastened with the others to the church. A good congregation was assembled, and the bride and bridegroom, children of peasant parents in the neighbourhood, were evidently well known to all. They each appeared to be about twenty-five years of age; and with the limited means at their disposal they had done their best to give to their appearance a neatness befitting the importance of the occasion. The bridegroom appeared in top-boots, velveteen trousers which in some places had lost their bloom, and an old-fashioned dark-blue coat. The bride wore a gown of bright blue stuff, and her head was covered with a cream-coloured woollen handkerchief fastened beneath her chin.

The wedding ceremony was not performed at the altar, but in the centre of the church. The priest received the couple at the door, led them to their place, and the chanting at once began. Two wax candles, each with a piece of red ribbon tied in a bow around it, were lighted and handed by the priest, one to the bridegroom, and the other to the bride; reminding both of the necessity for heedfulness and circumspection—keeping both eyes open, and taking a good look before they make the contemplated leap; and reminding each of the necessity to be candid as well as cautious, to beware of all suspicion of dissimulation or reserve, to let their minds to one another be honest as the light and open as the day, and so to plight their troth.

A large handkerchief was next spread out on the ground, and upon this handkerchief both were required to stand; expressive of the fact that henceforth they were to sail over the sea of life in the same boat, and share each other's lot. A Bible was then given them to kiss; signifying their acceptance of that book as the chart by which to regulate their course.

A couple of gold rings were now handed to the priest, who, having dipped them in holy water, gave one to each of the bridal pair. The man put his ring on the middle finger of the woman's right hand—a token that henceforth she belonged exclusively to him; and then the woman put her ring on the middle finger of the man's left hand, as a token that he belonged exclusively to her.

A gilded crown was then brought out and placed on the head of the bridegroom; proclaiming him the king of the new home. Before I had recovered from my surprise at this, another crown was brought and placed upon the head of the bride; proclaiming that, if her husband was to be king of the household, she was to be its queen.

The priest having next thrown a fold of his robe over their joined hands, grasped them, and led the man and woman three times round a table, on which lay a Bible and a crucifix; to teach them that the truth and the love of God must be the centre of all their movements. They then partook of the Sacrament of the Lord's Supper, to remind them of the price at which their happiness had been procured; the crucifix was held out for them to kiss, to signify that, in all the relationships of life, love for Christ must be supreme; then, to show that wedded love is also sacred, and a thing of which no one need be ashamed, before the whole congregation they kissed each other; and so the ceremony was complete.

The happy pair now left the church, and, amid the ringing of the bells and the congratulations of the people, went down to their little cottage by the lake, to spend, let us hope, a lifelong honeymoon.

I strolled out towards the open country after the wedding, infected naturally enough with the good-humour of the occasion, and one's nature responded cheerfully to the inspiring influence of the sunshine and the bracing Siberian air. But though the blue expanse above me was unsullied, there was a bank of cumulus on the horizon. It is seldom at this season that one sees a sky absolutely cloudless; and social life, even in remote Siberian villages, seems very much the same.

A man ran out of a cottage I had just passed, and asked me if I would oblige him by coming to see his son; and as the look upon his face told me that the case was an urgent one, I followed him at once.

The son referred to was a tall, well-built youth, within a few weeks of twenty years of age, and the eldest child of the family. He had been to the forest for a load of wood, and had returned with it to the village, when the horse became restive at the gate, and, in the effort to control him, by a sudden jerk a gun which the young man had with him in the cart went off, inflicting most serious injury upon his left arm and hand.

The mother—a kind but energetic-looking woman, nearly fifty years of age, and with hair already grey—had been watching the wedding in the church, wondering when she would have the privilege of witnessing a similar ceremony for her son. She returned just in time to see him carried wounded into the house.

A few neighbours had come in to help or to console, but they knew neither what to do nor what to say, and from the low doorway of the room, before I entered, I could see them and the members of the family standing in speechless horror, as if watching the approach of some dreadful apparition. And death was not very far away; his shadow was already creeping over the young man's face.

A sudden eagerness of hope lit up the face of the mother when she saw me, and with one authoritative word she swept the bystanders aside that I might not be impeded in my work. The wounded arteries being secured, life soon began again to struggle for the mastery, and the threatening spectre, seeing he was baffled, fled.

It seemed almost impossible to preserve the hand, but an attempt to do so was worth the while; so with stitches and bandages, and such splints and dressings as could be manufactured on the spot, the torn and contorted tissues were replaced in their position, and, thanks to the mother's care and the splendid health of the young man, both life and limb were saved.

I had no trouble after this in getting eggs and milk in Kamenrubeloff; and when I set out again on my journey, the whole family came to say farewell. The young man still had his arm in a sling, but otherwise seemed little the worse for his accident; the mother got far beyond my depth in Russian speech, but the look upon her face was my interpreter; and the father, though embarrassed in his manner, and less fluent than his wife, insisted upon taking me and my baggage to the steamer wharf, two or three miles from the village, with his own horse and cart.

CHAPTER VII

BY STEAMER FROM KHANKA TO THE AMOOR

THE clouds which I had seen gathering on the horizon brought a change of weather. A strong south wind began to blow, and by its warmth and vehemence, as it swept over the surface of Lake Khanka, speedily broke up the ice, and drove it in piled-up masses northward, leaving the southern half of that great sheet of water clear. As soon as the course was open, a steamer came over from the other side; and as several people had been waiting for it in the village for days and weeks, in a few hours it had booked its full complement of passengers, and was ready to start again.

We found the steamer waiting for us at a roughly-constructed wooden jetty a few miles from the village. It was a small craft, little more, indeed, than a steam-launch, and could barely accommodate the cabin passengers; those, therefore, who had deck tickets—soldiers, poor emigrants, and a few Coreans and Chinese—were placed, with the cargo, on a big lumbering barge, absurdly named the *Little Son*, and which was towed astern of us by a long hawser.

We loosed from our moorings an hour or two after dawn on a murky, miserable morning, and the outlook from our deck was a very dreary one. The few trees on the banks were leafless, the surface of the lake to the northward was a mass of ice, and over all rested a cold depressing haze. There were no other signs of navigation, and no boats of any kind in sight except our steamer and its barge. As the lake was forty miles across we could not see the other side, and the expanse of water which stretched away before us might have been mistaken for the sea; all the more so now because of the big waves which the wind had beaten up upon its surface, and which made our little steamer roll and pitch in a very uncomfortable way.

All day long we were tossing on the lake, and for several hours were out of sight of land; but in the afternoon, against the grey, cloud-covered sky, the farther shore appeared—a long, low bank, sentinelled by a few ragged, weather-beaten trees.

In trying to enter the Sungacha River, the principal outlet of the lake, we ran aground, and our little steamer had to be fairly lifted again into deep water by the leverage of long spars thrust under her keel from the barge. This so delayed us that it was nearly dark when we found our way into the river, and were able to anchor for the night.

We started again at daybreak, and it was astonishing to find that the river we were navigating was so small. Throughout its course of 350 miles, from the Khanka Lake to its confluence with the Usuri, the Sungacha is seldom more than a hundred feet wide; and it runs such a winding course that sometimes we had turned round a sudden bend, and were steaming westward, while our barge, which we could see through the shrubbery, abreast of us, was still running in the opposite direction. But the little river has a deep channel, and flows through a soft moorland country, so there was little fear of grounding; and if we did happen to run against the bank, it was the bank which suffered for it, and not the steamer.

Clumps of willow just breaking into leaf, and closely clustered to the water's edge, fringed the river on either side; and it was evidently a favourite haunt of water-fowl, for ducks, often in great flocks, flew up before our steamer at every turn. Some of them did not fly fast enough, and so were shot by an alert sportsman at our bow. They were picked up by a long-handled landing net, and passed over to the cook.

On all Siberian steamers wood is used for fuel, and, as this burns much more rapidly than coal, we had to stop at least once every day to fill our bunkers. This gave us an opportunity to ramble on the bank, and look more closely at the country, which, from its appearance outside the settlements, might never have been trodden by the foot of man. At intervals of from fifteen to twenty miles there were the post-horse stations to supply teams for sledges in the winter; at longer distances apart there were the wood stations to provide fuel for the steamers; and the people at these stations—a few yemschiks and wood-cutters—seemed to be the sole inhabitants. But the spring had come, and there was plenty of life about us in the bursting leaf-buds on the trees and the young grass covering the earth; and when I heard the lark singing as he soared, and saw the plovers tumble and heard their familiar cry, I forgot I was in such a solitary country and so far from home.

There were about a dozen other passengers upon the steamer, all of whom were Russian Government officials either in civil or military service. Five of them were quartered with me in the after-cabin—a small apartment measuring fourteen feet by ten. Here we lived and feasted, and here, on the settee around the table, we had to sleep at night, for there were no berths or separate cabins.

The steamer was moored against the bank at dark; and as there was not population enough in the neighbourhood to encourage thieves, and no other boat upon the river, we had no need of lights or watchmen, so towards midnight every lamp upon the steamer was put out, and everybody went to bed. The stillness and darkness ought to have helped us to slumber soundly, but there seemed to be always someone keeping vigil, and, at whatever hour of night I happened to awake, it was seldom that the black canopy around me was not relieved by one little Mars-like star low down on the horizon declaring itself at length, by some erratic movement, to be nothing but the burning tip of a cigarette.

Very polite are these Russian officers, but, though we

slept in the same room, we rose in the morning and put on our clothes without a single word to one another; and it was not until some water had been poured upon our hands by a sailor, and our toilet was complete, that we reassembled in the cabin, shook hands all round, and wished each other good-morning.

According to Russian custom we had two substantial meals a day—a dinner of three courses at noon, and a supper of one savoury dish at eight in the evening; also two lighter meals of tea and white bread and rusks, at seven in the morning and four in the afternoon. We had no butter with our bread—Russians are accustomed to eat it dry; and in Eastern and Central Siberia, though milk and curds and clotted cream are plentiful, butter and cheese are hardly known.

The ordinary bread used by the people is the black bread already described. It always has an acid taste, and a very small slice of it sufficed for me; but black bread with a little salt on it is very much relished by all classes of Russians. Wheaten bread in Siberia is a luxury only rarely to be obtained,—and that made of fine white flour is rarer still; it is known as French bread, and the people regard it very much as the English regard sponge-cake.

What tea-drinkers these Russians are! A Chinaman in Kamenrubeloff told me that one of his principal difficulties in associating with the people of this country was his inability to drink such quantities of tea. The Siberian easantry use what is called "brick-tea,"—*Kerpichni chai*

—which is simply pure tea-dust pressed by hydraulic power into slabs for convenience of transport. It is used in some parts of Siberia instead of money as a medium of exchange, and the value of a horse or cow or plot of land is estimated at so many bricks of tea. To prepare a drink of it, a piece is cut off with an axe and boiled for at least a quarter of an hour; simple infusion will not suffice to separate the hard-pressed particles.

It is only the poorer classes who habitually use this kind of tea, the dried leaf in its usual form being preferred by others. It is sometimes said that the best tea produced in China goes to Russia, but this is a mistake. The finest qualities of Chinese tea, which always yield a pale infusion, and are sold in native tea-shops at various prices, rising to upwards of five pounds sterling per pound avoirdupois, are entirely consumed by the Chinese; but of the coarser kinds, prepared expressly for foreign markets, and which mostly yield a dark infusion, probably the best is that which is carried overland through Siberia to Russia.

The tea the Russians drink is generally well diluted. A strong infusion having been made in a teapot, a small quantity (one or two tablespoonfuls) is poured into a half-pint goblet, which is then filled with boiling water from the samovar. A slice of lemon added is rightly considered an improvement, but milk or cream is never put in Russian tea; nor is it ever sweetened, though a lump of sugar is frequently placed on the table beside the tea-glass, and a small piece is bitten off it before each drink.

If four or five Russians sit round a samovar of gallon size, they seldom leave off drinking until the samovar is dry.

But tea is not the only beverage of the Russians in Siberia, nor by any means the strongest, and, great as is the quantity they drink, it is not easy to decide which the average Russian drinks most of—tea or vodka.

Two days after entering the Sungacha River, at one of the wood stations, a civil engineer in Government uniform wished to take a passage on our steamer; but he was so noisily and helplessly drunk that our captain had him placed with the steerage passengers on the barge. He had a big bold Siberian peasant woman with him, who was scolding him roundly. She was his "Siberian wife."

A considerable number of the Government officials appointed to Eastern Siberia leave their wives at home, not caring to subject them to the hardships of life and travel in this wild country. The term of service here is three years, which counts for promotion as the equivalent of five elsewhere, and for this period it is usual for these officials to engage a peasant woman of the country as housekeeper and wife. There is no attempt at concealment, nor does such proceeding involve any reflection whatsoever on a man's respectability. The woman is not deceived; she fully understands the temporary nature of the relationship, and is generally faithful to it.

Whether or not such a man desires from his wife in Europe a constancy greater than his own, he has usually sufficient sense of justice not to insist upon it, and an act of unfaithfulness which on the part of a concubine would inevitably lead a man to a duel with his rival, would on the part of a lawful wife be quietly ignored.

The civil engineer was sober enough by the next morning, and was admitted to the cabin of our steamer. I was surprised to find him such a modest, gentlemanly and cultured man. He held an important post in connection with the construction of the Siberian railway; belonged to a good family in St. Petersburg; had read extensively; and spoke English without suspicion of an accent. He professed to be of a decidedly religious turn, and told me that in this lonely region, where he was seldom within reach of a church, the study of the Scriptures was his principal relaxation and delight. I did not allude to the disgraceful condition in which I saw him on the previous day, though doing so would not, I think, have seriously offended him. In his judgment, drunkenness, unless too frequently repeated, was at worst but a pardonable indiscretion. But he seemed to have no idea that he himself had been drunk at all.

"I had a hard day yesterday," he said, "surveying a stretch of marshland, and from dawn to noon was up to my waist in mud. To save myself from getting fever, I went home and drank a pint of strong spirit, but I suppose I did not drink enough, for the fever came on in spite of it, and was so bad when I reached the steamer that the captain would not let me come on board. How this marsh fever does upset a man!"

At the confluence of the Sungacha and Usuri Rivers

we were transferred to another steamer, somewhat larger than the first, but with similar arrangements and accommodation. For the next five hundred miles our course lay down the latter river, which, with many windings east and west, makes its way northward to the Amoor. The Usuri is a much larger river than the Sungacha, and its water is clearer, but it flows through a similarly lonely and uncultivated country. Large fish darted from the bows of our steamer, and aquatic birds were still abundant. Flocks of ducks and geese frequently flew past us; and the inlets of the river and lagoon-like pools, of which we caught glimpses through the trees and shrubbery which fringed the river-bank, appeared to be covered with these and other kinds of waterfowl. At one of the wood-stations we heard of the depredations of a tiger. It had not only made havoc among the horses, but quite recently had killed two men. The district could ill afford this loss, for its human population is extremely small, the only signs of Western immigration being a few widely-severed settlements of Cossack woodcutters.

In addition to these Russian settlers, I saw at several wood-stations some interesting specimens of aboriginal tribes. A week or two later, on the banks of the Amoor, I saw them more frequently. Called by various names—Goldi, Orotchis, or Manegrs—according to the locality in which they settle, and some peculiarities of life, the natives of this region are all branches of the Tungusian tribe of Mongols, and are known to the Chinese by the name

Yü-pi ta-tsz, the meaning of which is roughly represented by the European designation, "*Fish-skin Tartars.*"

A queer-looking little people they are, with their characteristically Mongolian features—black hair and eyes, flat flabby noses, broad faces and prominent cheek-bones; and are so dwarfish in stature that a man of 5 feet 4 inches and a woman of 4 feet 10 inches are considered tall.

Their dwellings are huts of birch-bark; and half a dozen of them, sheltering as many families, and fifty or sixty dogs, make a Goldi or Orotchi village. These rude huts, though effective enough in protecting from the rain and snow, are too full of apertures to keep out the wind and cold; and, though the people have plenty of bear and reindeer skins to cover them, it is not surprising to find that painful rheumatic affections are very prevalent among them.

They appear to be as free as the Chinese from squeamishness with regard to what they eat, anything that will answer the purposes of food being, in an emergency, acceptable; but bear's flesh is their greatest luxury, and fish their most usual fare.

During the few months of their brief summer large quantities of fish are caught and dried for winter use. This dried fish, or *yukola*, is often ground into a sort of meal, which can be used instead of flour for making cakes. A most important commodity is yukola, both for man and beast; for towards the end of winter, when supplies of hay and barley are exhausted, even such strict vegetarians as cows and horses become carnivorous, and are glad of a good feed of fish-meal.

Most of the fish are caught in nets, but the children of the village are expected to contribute to the store with rod and line, and youngsters of eight or ten years old become skilful enough to land a fish of fifteen pounds. The twine of which the nets are made is prepared from the stalks of nettles which, in the summer-time, are found growing wild near every settlement. Before a net is used, it is boiled in reindeer blood to make it durable.

But it is not merely as food that fish are in such requisition, for the skins of fish are used not only to mend their houses, but even to make their clothes; and this is why these people have received the name of "Fish-skin Tartars." The dried fish-skin is first crumpled up by the hands into a ball, then rolled and pounded in a sort of wooden mortar, and when it has acquired the necessary suppleness it is sewn together and made up into trousers, tunics, aprons, and shoes, the soles of the latter being usually strengthened by a piece of reindeer hide.

The garments of most of the men I saw appeared to be made of salmon-skin; but fashionable ladies of the tribe selected, for their own and their children's clothing, skins with pretty stripes and markings; and after seeing one of these Orotchi nymphs in full fish-skin dress, if her face had only been a little prettier, I think I should henceforth have ceased to regard the mermaid as a myth.

These people have no literature or written language, and no wealth of historical tradition. They have a keen memory for landmarks, and can retrace their steps with unerring accuracy after a week's journey in the trackless forest; but they can remember little else, and a woman is seldom able to keep count of her children's age beyond five years.

Their family life is simple. Girls are usually married at from fifteen to sixteen, and boys at from eighteen to twenty years of age. As no females remain unmarried beyond girlhood, the range of selection for a man who desires a wife is a narrow one; but, having made his choice, he need have no fear of a refusal if he is able to pay to the girl's father the stipulated price, which is usually fifty sable-skins, a few pieces of silk, and a kettle.

There is no wilful polygamy among the Fish-skin Tartars, but, as all married women are entailed, involuntary polygamy is by no means rare. When a man dies, his widow becomes the wife of his next elder or younger brother, or, if he has no brother, of his nearest male relative; and the survivor of several brothers may have so many wives thus added to his own, that, however angelic they may be, he finds his little birch-bark hut uncomfortably crowded.

The Orotchis are proud of their children, and treat them just as kindly whether they are girls or boys. Babies are put to lie in birch-bark cradles, padded with moss and shavings, and which are suspended from the roof of the hut. Dangling over them, to amuse the child, and rattling as the cradles swing, are strings of teeth and claws of various wild animals. When the infant is a few months old a fish's head is given it to suck and cut its teeth upon, and in a little while it is ready for its first suit of fish-skin clothes.

The religion of these tribes is a form of the Shamanism which once prevailed throughout Siberia, and was the religion of the ancestors of the modern Turks before they became Mohammedans. They recognise a supreme divinity, whom they call Anduri; and two subordinate ones, Kamtchanga, the god of the dry land, and Yemu, the god of the sea.

It is believed that the two latter gods may, on special occasions, make themselves manifest in material form to men; but the supreme god, Anduri, remains always invisible, though he may, to the Shaman, directly reveal his will.

The Shaman in an Orotchi settlement is a sort of wizard priest, corresponding to the medicine-men of African and Polynesian tribes. He is consulted by the people with a view to finding lost articles, avoiding some threatened disaster, or foretelling the issue of some contemplated enterprise, but especially to drive away disease. His power to help is supposed to depend upon some special revelation from Anduri, to receive which the Shaman works himself into a frenzy, dances about frantically, shouts, screams, and beats himself until he falls exhausted to the ground. In the dream which follows, Anduri is supposed to supply the necessary information, and on the morrow the Shaman communicates it to his client.

If the case be medical, the remedy usually prescribed is the construction of a rough wooden image of a wild beast or a man, its suspension from a tree in the neighbourhood of the Shaman's hut, and liberal supplies of oil and yukola to be placed before the image every evening, for it to feed upon in the darkness of the night. In the morning the bowls are always found empty, ready for a fresh supply. If recovery ensues, it is believed that the evil spirit of the disease has gone out of the patient into the wooden image, as the devils from the maniac at Gadara went into the herd of swine. If the sufferer dies, the Shaman, of course, declares that his directions with regard to the construction of the image and its nourishment have not been duly carried out.

These people believe that the soul is immortal, and that it remains in its old haunts for a fortnight after death; during which period, therefore, the place of the deceased is always left vacant in the family circle, and at meal-times the bowl and chop-sticks are placed before it. The corpse is laid in a pine-wood coffin, which is not buried, but fixed on a wooden stand a few feet above the ground, and a small birch-bark hut is constructed over it. Sepulture is considered so important, that when the body of a relative who has been drowned cannot be recovered, a rough wooden image of him is coffined and entombed instead.

The only public religious festival now observed among these people is the "Bear Feast," which usually takes place in the middle of winter, as an expression of gratitude for success in hunting or for some other benefit received. The ceremony consists in leading round from hut to hut a three-year-old bear, which has been caught and fattened for the purpose. The bear is decked with ribbons and ornaments, and is kept under control by ropes attached to its body, neck, and forepaws, and held tight in opposite directions. At each hut visited a feast is provided for both bear and people; and at the end of the third day the animal is tied to a tree, and shot at with bows and arrows by the best marksmen of the tribe. If they fail to kill it at seventy yards, they come gradually nearer until they succeed. When the bear is dead, pine-log fires are kindled, the flesh is cut up and roasted, and all the people gather round and feast until there is nothing left.

The favourite occupation of the Orotchis is sable-hunting, and almost all the adult male population is engaged in it from the end of September to the beginning of May. Far away to the eastward, as we steamed down the Usuri, we could see long ranges of mountains. They are very imperfectly known to European geographers, but are generally grouped together under the name Sikhotaalin. Among the wild jungles and almost impenetrable forests which cover this region is the Orotchis' hunting-ground.

Each Orotchi selects his own district, and goes out to the hunt alone. As soon as he reaches the confines of the forest, he stops to ask the favour of the gods upon his enterprise. To Anduri, the Supreme, whom the poor hunter regards as too great to need or to accept an offering, he simply prays; but he seeks to propitiate Kamtchanga, the god of the forest, by a gift of fish-meal cakes. Then he continues his journey until he comes upon a stream, when he begins at once to ply his craft. As shot-holes in a sable-skin lessen its value, the shrewd hunter tries to capture the animals by various kinds of snares. Cutting down a number of pine saplings, he proceeds to lay them across the stream at intervals of a dozen or more yards, having first fixed in the centre of each a spring noose. The sables trying to make use of these saplings as bridges in crossing from one bank to the other, can hardly fail to get the slip-knot round their necks.

When the stream is frozen this method fails, for the sables are not likely to try the saplings when, on the ice, they can cross the river where they like. But the experienced sable-hunter can adapt his methods to the altered circumstances, and, watching quietly until he sees a sable run into a hollow tree, he quickly adjusts a net over the opening, and then drives the frightened sable into it by loud shouting, and by beating against the bark with a club. Other kinds of trap and snare are also used; and the hunter does not hesitate to shoot a sable with a small-bore rifle when he can obtain it in no other way.

Though mainly in pursuit of sable, he has ever a keen eye for other marketable spoil; and fox, otter, muskdeer, wild boar, bear, elk, and reindeer often reward his toil. A skilful Orotchi hunter will secure in a good season as many as seventy sables, thirty foxes, and seventy-five head of other game.

These native Siberian hunters have great powers of

endurance. The only provision they take with them on their excursions is a few pounds of fish-meal cakes and a piece of brick-tea. In addition to these things they have a kettle, flint and steel, rifle and ammunition, bows and arrows, and an assortment of nets and snares. They go on from day to day, plunging deeper and deeper into the forest, and never think of turning back until their stock of victuals is exhausted; the return journey, though encumbered perhaps with half a hundredweight of skins in addition to their gear, and occupying the best part of a week, being performed by them without any food at all.

The Orotchis and their kindred tribes were once very numerous in this region, but since the advent of Europeans their numbers have seriously declined. They are all more or less the victims of oppression—oppression arising not so much from the harshness of Russian law as from the irrepressible cupidity of the tax collector. The tribute fixed by Government is a rouble and a half per man, to be paid in sable-skins, but the collector will never accept the skins at more than a third of their market value. In the interests of the aborigines, the Government has made it illegal to supply them with intoxicating drink; but this only exposes them to new exactions, for the itinerant Chinese or Manchu spirit-vendor still carries the forbidden poison from one village to another, and demands an extortionate price for it as compensation for the risk of his defiance of the law. In this and other ways the conditions of their life are becoming harder and more impracticable every year, and in a few decades the race will be extinct.[1]

A little after dawn one morning, about a week after leaving Khanka Lake, we saw ahead of us against the sky a great mountain-bluff, on its western side rising abruptly from the river, but continuous to the eastward with a low range of hills. There was a silver streak along its summit, and, as we drew nearer, this streak resolved itself into a line of low, white-painted cottages—a Siberian village, so it seemed; but the captain of our steamer told us that it was the city of Khabarofka, the metropolis of the Maritime and Amoor provinces of Siberia.

The Governor-General of these provinces resides here; but the office happened to be vacant at the time of my visit, Baron Korf, the last Governor-General, having died a few months before. His son, a fine young Cossack officer, had just arrived from St. Petersburg to take his widowed mother home.

Here it is that the hunters of Far Eastern Siberia find a market for their furs, and sometimes more than twenty thousand pounds worth of sable-skins alone have passed through the city in one season. It will be a busy grain-mart some day, for around it are tens of thousands of acres of virgin soil waiting only for the husbandmen.

It was a stiff climb to the top of the great rocky platform on which the city stands, and it did not, on a

---

[1] An interesting résumé of facts respecting the social life of the Orotchis, from Margaritoff and other Russian writers, is contained in a paper by M. F. A. Fraser, published in the *Journal* of the China Branch of the Royal Asiatic Society.

nearer view, look much more like a city than when I saw it from below—except perhaps in size, for it has such wide streets, and its single-storied wooden houses have been built so far apart, that when Khabarofka has a population of 100,000—forty or fifty times the number of its present one—it need not cover a more extensive area than it does to-day.

The houses look neat and clean, but everything else is in the rough. Some planking has been laid down on the side-walk, but there has been no metalling of the streets, which are simply enclosed portions of the moor. The ground in the centre has been broken up by the droskies, but on either side their track grass was growing, and a few wild flowers, and I suppose it was the sense of loneliness which made one's heart swell so at finding among them a cluster of homely dandelions.

The city has, in addition to a couple of small churches, a fine new cathedral. It is hexagonal in shape, and has five towers, each covered with a light green cupola, and surmounted by a gilded cross.

The cathedral stands away from the houses on the western extremity of the rocky platform, which is also its highest point, having a fall to the river, almost precipitous, of over six hundred feet. The situation is an ideal one, it commands such an extensive prospect. The vast plains which spread themselves out on the other side of the river are part of the empire of China. The rest of the city is hidden from those plains by the contour of the bluff, but the cathedral is a conspicuous landmark, and anywhere within a score of miles it should be plainly visible.

Old Cathay is here brought into the closest contact with Western civilization. The Russian advance has been checked by the river, but only for a moment; that river will soon be crossed; and if Chinese watchers in the distance are aware of the power which is invading them, and can foresee its victory, it should be some relief to the gloom of their forebodings to see in the van of the invading force a Christian church.

The civilization of Russia may be less highly developed than our own, but it is very far ahead of the civilization of the Chinese; and what is spoken of as Russian encroachment in Eastern Asia may be not only the best thing for the welfare of our race, but, in the nature of things, inevitable. The healthy tree must take up and assimilate whatever is nutritious in the decaying vegetation round about it; light cannot co-exist with darkness, nor heat with cold; and when two such races as the Russians and Chinese are brought so close together, these claimants of the future and dreamers of the past cannot both be masters; sooner or later a struggle for supremacy—not of necessity by force of arms—must arise, and in that struggle the fittest will survive.

I was sitting alone on the edge of the cliff, on the evening after my arrival in the city, thinking of these problems. The cathedral was at my back, far below me was the river, and beyond it the Manchurian plains, bounded in the far distance by a low range of hills, behind which the sun was sinking fast. Suddenly there fell upon my ears the inspiring strains of a fine military band. The players were hidden from me by a clump of trees, but the beautiful blending of sweet sounds flowed into the current of my thought; and as the waves of this martial symphony rose and fell, challenge and defiance now softening into pity and now swelling again into exultation and triumph, it seemed to me like the march music of that Christian civilization which some of us believe is destined to regenerate China and overspread the earth.

CHAPTER VIII

UP THE AMOOR

WINDING half-way round the foot of the Khabarofka bluff, beneath the shadow of its northern wall, the Usuri River meets with the Amoor; and thence, in united strength, the two confluent rivers roll down towards the coast-range mountains to force a passage through them to the sea. Our way to Europe lies westward, up the stream to the wild table-lands, where the Amoor musters its forces for the sweep it makes through these lowland plains. It is indeed a noble river. Here at Khabarofka, nearly eight hundred miles from its mouth, it is half a mile in width, and is navigable for a farther distance of twice as far again.

The steamers for ascending the Amoor are larger and more comfortable than those on the Usuri; and fortunately I had not long to wait for one, the steamer on which I took my passage leaving Khabarofka the day after that of my arrival.

There were eight of us in the after-cabin, and my companions were a set of good-natured, careless young men, most of them in Government employ. They spent the whole day playing baccarat, had hardly patience enough to desist while the table was cleared for meals, and played far on into the night. However small their stakes, several of the players in the course of a few days lost all they had. When this happened to one, he slunk from the table and went up on deck; and there we saw him sitting, hour after hour, with his elbows on his knees and his chin on his hands, heedless of his fellow-passengers, heedless of the scenery on the banks, heedless even of the dinner-bell, and apparently interested only in one little portion of the deck, at which he continued to stare vacantly.

We all live and sleep in the one cabin, as on the two previous steamers; but on neither of them was the discomfort of the arrangement so intrusive as it is on this. Our gamblers sat up too late at night for the cabin to be made tidy after they were asleep, and, when the steward came in at eight o'clock in the morning to set the breakfast, he found the table littered from one end to the other with pieces of bread, tea-glasses, vodka-bottles, playing-cards, candles, hats, tooth and hair brushes, towels, soap, shaving apparatus, books, matches, cigarette-ashes, and perhaps the clothes of one or two who were not yet dressed.

It was a relief to go up on deck and look at the river, or even at the virgin forest on its banks, for, with all its wild luxuriance, there was in that tangled mass of vegetation no suggestion of confusion. Masses of ice were floating down the river, and their white, gleaming surface was all the more conspicuous, because the water of the

Amoor, stained with pine leaves, is of a dark-brown colour, like that of a peat-moss stream. The little gullies between the hills were filled with compressed snow, moving down slowly, like miniature glaciers, towards the river. The banks, which rose on either side above the snow-filled gorges, wherever clear of forest, were covered with rhododendrons, now in full bloom; the bright red patches extending downward to the green willows on the margin of the river, and upward to the dark pine trees, which stood between them and the sky.

Immense shoals of salmon were making their way with us up the stream, and they seemed to think so little of the long voyage from the sea—a thousand miles and more—which they had already made, and of the still longer one which yet lay before them, opposed by a strong adverse current, that in sheer exuberance of energy they kept leaping their whole length from the water as they went along.

Lovers of the gentle craft could hardly wish for better fishing waters than those of the Amoor. On its banks, beneath the cliffs of Khabarofka, anglers were always to be seen in the day-time, and, though provided only with rough home-made rods and lines, everyone who had been fishing for any length of time had a good basket of fish—pike, bream, carp, perch, with several other kinds of fish not found in British waters. Salmon, though usually caught by means of nets, are frequently taken by the angler with sunken bait, but fly-fishing in this part of Siberia appears to be unknown. Sturgeon are very plentiful, and one of 20 lbs. could be bought for about a shilling. To this family belongs the Kalooga—the largest fish in the Amoor. It often attains a weight of 2800 lbs., the head alone of such a fish weighing 360 lbs.

Fish are so abundant in this river that even dogs have learned to catch them, and in walking on the bank a

ON THE AMOOR.

native of the country is not at all surprised to find one of these canine fishers, dripping wet, and making a meal of a fine salmon which he has seized by the head and dragged out of the water.

At noon, on the fifth day of our voyage, we arrived at Blagovestchensk, a town whose appearance is by no means so imposing as its name. It straggles along the left bank of the Amoor for several miles, but its wooden houses are so small, and are built so far apart, that the total population cannot much exceed twelve thousand. There are hills in the distance, but the country in the immediate neighbourhood is flat and uninteresting, and there is nothing to attract the visitor either in the town or its surroundings.

Yet Blagovestchensk is regarded by the people as, next to Vladivostock, the most important town—or rather city —in Far Eastern Siberia; and there is even a sort of see-Mecca-and-die tone in the conversation of settlers respecting it. This extravagance is excusable enough, for the area of the province is so vast, and its total population is so small, that a city with upwards of a myriad of people in it is of as much relative importance to the country as its largest cities are to England.

But, apart from such considerations, the simplicity of its appearance cannot conceal the fact that Blagovestchensk is a prosperous little settlement. Its numerous, well-stocked stores, the quality of the wares exposed for sale, the comparatively high prices which they command, and the evident contentment of its inhabitants, are plain proof of the sufficiency of its resources. So enlightened and enterprising are its citizens, that they are taking steps to establish here a Bacteriological Institute for the inoculation of horses against a form of anthrax which is very prevalent among the equine population of the country, and is known as the "Siberian Plague."

Commercially, this city owes its importance to its situation near the confluence of the Zeya with the Amoor, for on the banks of that little river have been discovered some of the richest gold-fields in the empire. The mining is mainly in the hands of three large Russian companies; but there are also many syndicates, and even individual diggers working on their own account. The work is at present confined entirely to alluvial deposits; and the yield of gold which passes through Blagovestchensk averages 200,000 ounces every year.

The city is politically important as the capital of the great Amoor province. It has a large military depôt, and in the city and its neighbourhood there is abundant evidence of the energy and sagacity with which Russia is establishing her power in this most easterly part of her dominions. It is only a few tens of years since she gained possession of this province, and though for upwards of a thousand miles there is only the breadth of the Amoor between the territory of Russia and of China, the defence of this extensive frontier is, on the Russian side, complete.

In addition to infantry, whose numbers I could not ascertain, there are in this province 30,000 Cossack regulars, and twice as many more reserves, who, with their families, are posted along the river in little townships twenty miles apart, and who support themselves by the cultivation of plots of land which have been granted to them by the Government, on condition that each man keeps himself and a good horse in readiness for active service at a moment's call.

The Chinese territory on the other side appeared, over extensive areas, to be neither protected nor inhabited. Whatever might be the nature of the country, whether pine-clothed mountains or rolling plains, for hundreds of miles there was no town or village, nor even house, to be seen. It looked like a veritable No-man's Land. During the last few years the Pekin Government has made some attempt to establish colonies along the Manchurian frontier, but with indifferent success. There is one fair-sized town, called Sakalin, nearly opposite to Blagovestchensk, and within a few miles above and below are a few small villages; but, with these exceptions, the only signs of human life on the Chinese bank of the Amoor—and these but rarely — were the wigwams of some wandering Tartars.

The transference of this extensive, valuable, but altogether undeveloped territory from Chinese to Russian rule is only a question of time; and let us hope, in the interests of humanity, that the time will not be long.

On a fine calm evening, with the sun just setting in the west, and the moon rising shyly in the east to peep at him, we loosed from our moorings and recommenced our run up the Amoor. We had been transferred to another steamer, longer and broader than the previous one, but of lighter draught, and propelled by a single paddle-wheel at the stern. In the second cabin I had with me an entirely new set of fellow-passengers. There were too many of us for the size of our saloon, but my companions were far more interesting than those I had left behind; and as they were not in bondage night and day to baccarat, we had diversity of occupation, with plenty of entertaining and instructive conversation, and so our life was less monotonous.

No other European people that I know, and least of all the English, are equal to the Russians in the freedom with which in a promiscuous company they can make themselves at home with one another; and, now that serfdom is abolished, there is probably less of hereditary exclusiveness in Russia than in any other country in the world. We had no barge in tow after we entered the Amoor, so first and second cabin and steerage passengers had all to be accommodated on the steamer; and a very miscellaneous company we were. But we got on very well together. Natural barriers were respected, but there was no attempt by those on the other side to buttress them, or to enlarge the area they enclosed by artificial ones.

In the first saloon were a dozen military officers of high rank. One of them was a General Gemelman, over sixty years of age, but still hale and active. He seems to enjoy this rough Siberian service, and, after spending six or seven hours in the saddle, says he thinks nothing of responding to some urgent message by another ride of twenty miles on the same day. He did not know English, but was fond of talking French, and we had many an hour's interesting conversation. He first saw active service in the Crimea, where he made the acquaintance of General Gordon, and commenced with him a lifelong friendship. To these two, "Love your enemies" was evidently not an impracticable command. The last letter received from Gordon was written from Khartoum, only a few months before its fall.

Another noteworthy passenger was the colonel of a Cossack regiment—a man in the prime of life, and a splendid specimen of masculine physique. He spoke English fluently, and was full of information about the history and resources of Siberia. There appeared to be no reserve whatever in his conversation, and he seemed ready to talk with the utmost freedom on all sorts of subjects; but in reality he was ever on his guard, and the slightest and most delicate suggestion or inquiry with regard to the probable extension of Russian territory on the Chinese side of the river invariably led to an adroit change of subject, or to an abrupt termination of the conversation. One could not but entertain a high respect for the wariness and self-control which enabled this officer to associate such perfect reticence with so much frankness and affability.

A number of younger officers were with me in the second-class saloon, and these I got to know more intimately, but acquaintance only confirmed my first opinion with regard to their courtesy and culture. One of them, indeed, had a lurking suspicion that I was a British spy, and he shook his head knowingly whenever he caught sight of me. This suspicion probably persisted to the end, but with ever-lessening strength and definiteness. The suspicious one was never impolite; and anything like snobbishness in any of them I never saw. They were open and communicative on all but forbidden topics, and were very well informed, not only on such subjects as the geology, fauna, and flora of Siberia, but even on English literature. In the course of my journey I met with hundreds of men in their position, and was not surprised to find a few boors among them; but, taking one with another, it is only just to say, that in education and refinement; in frankness, intelligence, and common-sense; in uniform courtesy of demeanour; and, above all, in freedom from bondage to the absurd conventionalisms of caste, Russian military officers appear to be at least the equals of any other members of their profession in the world.

We had other cabin companions of a rougher mould, including a Mohammedan Tartar, named Aplin, who had been down the river to purchase hides; and three horse-dealers from Tomsk, who had just brought a drove of four hundred horses to Blagovestchensk for the Russian Government, and now were returning home. In appearance these were Russians, but they told me that their nationality was Ivry, and asked if I had ever met any of their race in England. The name was strange to me, and I could not for a time imagine to what portion of the world or to what people it referred; but one day, when leaning on the bulwarks of our steamer gazing at some passing scene, I quoted in soliloquy a passage from the Hebrew Bible, which a friendly rabbi once taught me, and, being overheard by one of the horse-dealers, he ran up to me excitedly and said, "So you are Ivry, too?" Honesty compelled me to disclaim the suggested kinship, but I knew now that Ivry was only another name for Jew.

I saw many of these people afterwards,—both exiles and free emigrants,—and some of them appeared to be very estimable persons; but in most of the Russian Jews to be met with in Siberia, craft and cupidity are so conspicuous, that though they do not of course justify their persecutions, they do much to explain them. The Ivry always complained bitterly of the treatment they received, and when I asked them why they were thus treated, they invariably replied, "Because we crucified Jesus."

This historic fact, ancient as it is, would be likely enough to feed the flame of resentment among the lower orders of a people whose Christianity is of the Russian type; but for the kindling of the flame we need not look for so remote a cause—we have it in the heartless avarice which marks the monetary dealings of this people with the Russian peasantry. Released from serfdom within the last thirty years, these peasants have not yet learned to manage prudently their own affairs. When money is needed to work their land, the simplest way is to get it from the Jews, and they thus fall an easy prey to the pitiless exactions of these unscrupulous money-lenders. The property of one after another of the peasant farmers of a district being appropriated by the usurers, the wrath of the people at length breaks out. The fire once kindled, all that is bad in Jewish reputation and history becomes so much fuel to support it, and a terrible vengeance is inflicted.

Our third-class passengers had to make themselves as comfortable as they could upon the deck. There were about two hundred of them, the majority being through-passengers; but a few joined and left us at some of the river-side wood-stations. Among these transient deck passengers were several *popes*, this name being in Russia the designation of ordinary priests. At various towns and villages upon the way, as well as on the steamer, I had the privilege of frequent interviews with men of this fraternity. They are easily distinguished from the rest of the people by their striking appearance; their hair, which is allowed to grow as long as a woman's, being parted in the middle, and hanging loosely down their back; and their robe, which is often of a light-blue colour, being long enough to reach almost to their feet.

Though the people here esteem so highly the church and its services, they do not seem to entertain any special veneration for their priest. But if they do not reverence him like the Irish, they neither laugh at him like the French, nor shun him like many of the English. They believe that priestly functions are important, just as we believe the delivery of letters is important; but, apart from those functions, a pope is of no more consequence to the people of Siberia than a postman off duty is to us. But though a pope of the Russian Church is on ordinary occasions treated by the people with mere ordinary courtesy, like an ordinary man, he is regarded by the Government as an essential part of the machinery of State, and is protected from injury and insult by most rigorous laws.

Personally, the popes of Siberia appear to be a very

simple-minded set of men; knowing little except theology, and not much, I should think, of that. I never met one who could speak any other language than his own; and their education as a class compares very unfavourably with that of Russian naval and military officers, and still more unfavourably with that of the priests of the Church of Rome.

Their moral character is held to be without reproach. Each is supposed to be "the husband of one wife," and, according to the Greek Church interpretation of that apostolic phrase, he is not allowed to marry again though the first wife is dead. But the letter of this requirement is evidently believed to be more important than its spirit, and a widower-pope, though forbidden to re-marry, may take a mistress with impunity. When little children are left upon his hands who require a mother's care, the poor pope is almost forced to such a compromise; but in any case such an irregular alliance is not formed surreptitiously, —the relationship is recognised by the parishioners without any reflection upon their pope's virtue or respectability, and there is no more reserve in speaking of one woman as a pope's mistress than there is in speaking of another as a pope's wife.

The priests on our steamer were only travelling short distances, and were never more than a day or two on board; but most of our steerage passengers were time-expired soldiers going home, and they remained with us throughout our three or four weeks' run. They had no accommodation but the deck, with an awning to protect them from the rain, but with no shelter from the wind and frost. In the sunshine at noonday the air was comfortably warm, but with masses of ice upon the river, and of snow upon its banks, it was bitterly cold at night. No food was provided for the deck passengers, who had to be content with what they had brought with them or what they could purchase at the wood-stations; and not being allowed to cook on board, at meal after meal their only fare was old toasted bread and coarse rusks dipped in hot tea, with the occasional luxury of hard-boiled eggs.

These Russian soldiers were exceedingly well behaved, and were models of patient endurance—sleeping on the bare deck, eating the plainest food, working like slaves at the wood-stations carrying fuel to the steamer, with the prospect of two thousand miles of hard walking when their voyage on the river is completed; yet they never complained. They did their best to keep themselves and each other cheerful; whenever there was anyone to fiddle for them they were always ready for a dance, and often after sunset they tried to keep themselves warm till bedtime by singing ballads, in the choruses of which everyone appeared to join.

Some of the soldiers were married, and had their wives and children with them; and every afternoon we saw these soldiers and their wives, utterly regardless of their own personal comfort, carefully rearranging their boxes and bundles on the deck, so as to form snug recesses in which their little ones might safely sleep while the chill night winds blew.

Steamers on the Amoor, like those on the Usuri, use wood as fuel, a fact which is as evident to passengers on deck as to firemen in the engine-room, for not only is an awning necessary, but it must be made of sheet-iron; and abaft the funnel there are frequently repeated showers of red-hot charcoal, in pieces larger than a hazel nut. At night, when we happen to be steaming, they illuminate the ship like showers of falling stars.

It is said that springs of mineral oil have been recently discovered on the island of Saghalien, and that very soon petroleum will take the place of wood in the firing of these steamers. Such a substitution will mean a considerable economy both of space and time, for the quantity of wood required to keep up steam is enormous; and I was surprised to find that the continual demand had not yet made any perceptible inroad upon the forests of this region. With wood filling our bunkers, and stacked up in every available space upon the deck, in less than twenty-four hours we had to stop again at a wood-station to replenish our supply,

At each of these wood-stations was a settlement of ten or more log-huts, the settlers not only cutting wood for the steamers, but rearing a few cattle, and sometimes cultivating small plots of land. No sooner was our steamer moored, than the wives and daughters of the settlers, with their short print-dresses, handkerchief-bound heads and bare feet, came to the top of the bank above us with bottles of milk, basins of clotted cream, loaves of bread, and baskets of eggs. The steamer was the only market available for the sale of their farm produce, but they generally found there a sufficient number of purchasers.

Board was not included in our passage money, but was supplied to order by the ship's steward at a fixed charge per day. It was, however, much cheaper for each passenger to provide board for himself, and on this steamer all except the Government officials did so. We could not in this way have much variety, being limited to such provisions as we could carry with us, and the few simple articles of diet to be obtained at the wood-stations. There were so many passengers on our steamer—the first this season to ascend the river—that the demand for milk and eggs was in excess of the supply, and the only way to be sure of getting any was to be among the first ashore. This often meant a long jump from the steamer, and a quick run up a steep bank, but I generally managed to reach the sale-ground before the last bottle of milk had gone.

One evening at dusk we found ourselves running for several miles under a gigantic cliff, which rose from the left bank of the river almost perpendicularly to the height of several hundred feet. In the twilight it was impossible to observe its structure, but it appeared to be of a pale grey colour, and at the height of about a hundred feet from the river was cut by two horizontal strata of some black substance which looked like coal. On the face of the cliff, at various elevations, were ridges which we should have believed to be little more than a finger's-breadth in size, had we not observed the rows of fir-trees which found footing there.

There are few, if any, rivers in the world whose scenery surpasses that of some parts of the Amoor. As we ascended, it became wilder and more romantic every mile, until at length we seemed to be enclosed on every side by mountain ranges and primeval forest.

Waking very early one morning, and finding the cabin stuffy—as it well might be, with every window closed and twelve of us sleeping round the table—I gathered my rugs around me and went up on to the deck. The air, though intensely cold, was pure and bracing, and its inhalation refreshed one like new wine. A fog was resting on the river, and for a time this gauzy veil of overhanging mist was all that I could see, but as the sun came nearer the horizon the veiling became thinner and more transparent, and soon the shadowy outline of some bold headland loomed out upon us through the haze. As the sun rose higher the outline became more distinct, other bluffs began to show themselves; and when at length the sun broke out, the mist had vanished, and we found ourselves cowering in the midst of a Titanic concourse of hills and mountains, the nearer ones clad in a shaggy vesture of virgin forest, and stooping, as it were, with age, while their brothers in the purple distance seemed to stand on tiptoe to peer over the shoulders of the rest. But it was not at us they gazed; in the light of a new day they were looking forth upon the Infinite, and were rapt in such absorbing contemplation that our little steamer and its puny freight were far beneath their notice.

We thought we were alone upon the river, until our attention was arrested by an object floating towards us with the current, and which proved to be a pine-log raft, upon which a company of Siberian peasants were making their way to some distant settlement. They had built for themselves a small log-hut, and planted young fir trees round it, whose roots or severed trunks must have reached into the water, for the foliage looked as fresh as if the saplings were in their native soil. There was an oar for steering, but there were no means of propulsion, the stream carrying the men along as fast as they wished to go; so they had leisure to enjoy themselves, and in their tunics of Turkey-red they lounged in all sorts of easy attitudes upon the raft as it drifted past us down the river.

Sometimes a thickly-wooded group of islands appeared ahead of us, breaking up the channel of the river, and as we steamed between them it seemed as if the great Amoor had dwindled to a small fishing-stream; but past the islands it broadened out again into a magnificent expanse of water.

Siberian sunsets, if less gorgeous than those of hotter climes, are often exquisitely beautiful, and none are more so than those which are observed amidst the scenery of the Amoor. As our course lay westward we saw them to advantage, and one evening the colours of the sky— azure, pink, and orange—were reproduced in all their splendour on the surface of the river, the light of heaven marked off from its reflection by a line of forest-covered hills.

These hills seemed to gather closer round us as the sun went down; and when the darkness was too dense for us to see our course, or the reaches immediately above us were difficult to navigate, our steamer was moored for the night against the bank. This gave our poor deck passengers the only opportunity they had of getting a genuine hot meal. They could nŏt cook on board, and during our short stay at a wood-station they were busy carrying fuel to the steamer; but stopping for the night gave them a chance, of which they so quickly availed themselves that in a few minutes our decks were quite deserted.

Those who were not engaged in cooking climbed higher up the wooded steep, and sat there singing wild, cheery choruses which echoed among the hills. We could not see the singers, for the whole scene was wrapped in darkness, save in a few spots below where the forest was lit up by blazing logs, around which, their faces glowing with the flame, were a group of eager men, each with a pine-branch, holding in fishrod-fashion his kettle of millet and potatoes over the fire.

An hour later the fires were out, and all the rest of the passengers and crew were in their beds. The forest-covered mountains stood black against the sky, their shadows lay black upon the river, and all was still as death, save for the occasional splash of a fish or a flight of nocturnal birds. Then I began to shiver with the cold, and remembered that it was time to creep under the blankets and go to sleep.

We went on all night whenever the sky gave light enough for us to see our way; and sometimes, when the stars were dim, we found the river lit up for us by widespread forest-fires. How, in these unpopulated districts, such fires are kindled no one seems to know; perhaps by a flash of lightning, or a spark from a passing steamer, or the smouldering brands of a camp-fire left by some careless hunter; but, however caused, when once started these conflagrations are beyond control. They burn for weeks, and spread over the forest-land for miles. One night we passed through a region where the whole mountain-side seemed to be in flames. We had seen other forest-fires before, but none on such a scale as this. It took our steamer nearly an hour to pass it. We heard the flames roar as they attacked new areas of stubble, and crackle among the prostrate trees; while the sky above, and the surrounding river, and the awe-struck faces of the people on our deck, reflected the red light.

The underwood and saplings were the first to yield, and in the midst of the space covered by their burning ashes we sometimes saw a group of cedars—giants of the forest—still standing defiantly amidst their fallen brothers, as if to challenge the advance of the destroyer. Their shaggy forms looked black as night against the glowing background, save where, like fiery serpents, the flames twined round their trunks and branches; and with a clinging persistency which told us that in this Laokoon struggle, the serpents, however desperately resisted, will secure their prey.

The night seemed unusually dark when the burning forest had been left behind, and the stars seemed almost afraid to shine. But the officers on watch said they could make out the course, and we should not have dropped anchor had we not been compelled to do so by an exciting incident among our passengers.

On the morning of that day a soldier had fallen overboard. The alarm was given while we were at breakfast, and, rushing from the table to the deck, I could see at some distance astern of us the man's head above the water. No life-belt was thrown to him, and though the engines were promptly stopped, and a boat was at once lowered, the strong current had carried the man half a mile away before the rescuing party left the steamer. With a glass, I could still see the soldier swimming for his life, but just before the boat got to the place he disappeared. We all gave him up for lost, and were not a little surprised, when the boat's crew returned, to find that they had the soldier with them. Owing to the clearness of the water, the drowning man had been still visible to his rescuers after he had sunk, and catching his garments with a boat-hook they hauled him on board. He was quite unconscious, and more dead than alive when brought to the steamer, but with a little medical attention he soon revived.

In confirmation of the adage that troubles seldom come to us singly, a little before midnight, on that same day, the cry was raised that a man was missing. Again it was a soldier, and, as a long search had been made for him before the announcement was given, there could be little doubt of its truth. It was this report which led to the sudden dropping of our anchor an hour or two after the great forest-fire was passed. Of course we could see nothing, and though profound stillness followed the stopping of the engines, for some time nothing could be heard; but at length there reached us a faint but distinctly human call. It seemed to come up the river, and from a distance of several miles, but our whole ship's company united in sending back a call of recognition, and then the boat was lowered. We watched its lamp-light fading in the distance until it became invisible, and then waited in suspense for it to reappear. More than an hour we waited, but at length the boat was again alongside, and it brought the missing soldier safe and sound. He must have been an unusually expert swimmer, for he had been in the ice-cold water for upwards of an hour, and had succeeded in taking off, while swimming, not only his heavy sheepskin coat, but even his top-boots.

We had now reached the lower terrace of the table-land, 3000 feet above the sea, and still we were ascending. The river was now called the Shilka, for it does not take the name of the Amoor until it joins the Argun, some 1600 miles above its entrance to the sea. The Argun runs along the frontier of Mongolia, and when we passed its confluence with the Shilka, and continued our course westward along the latter river, we no longer had

Chinese territory on our left hand; the country on both sides of us was Russian.

The banks of the Shilka were mountainous and densely wooded; but in some parts the ranges receded from the river, leaving on its banks wide fields of grass-land. These fields were generally the sites of settlements, and in one of them we saw a convict station—a big pile of buildings, white and clean, and cheerful outside, but dreary enough within; for the penal laws of Russia are intended to be "a terror to evil-doers," and its convict system an object-lesson to enforce the truth that "the way of transgressors is hard." The pity of it is that the innocent so often suffer with the guilty.

On the following morning we reached Stretensk, a small town on the right bank of the river, the head of its navigable portion; and so the termination of our voyage. More than a month had passed since we left Lake Khanka, and we were now two thousand miles above the mouth of the Amoor. For the next two thousand miles, with the exception of one day's steamer trip across Lake Baikal, we must travel again by tarantass.

THE SHILKA RIVER AND THE TOWN OF STRETENSK.

CHAPTER IX

FROM STRETENSK TO LAKE BAIKAL, BY TARANTASS

It was about nine in the morning when our steamer moored, and at once there was a general rush to the post-horse station to secure conveyances. I did not take part in it, for the fifteen horses kept here were not sufficient for the military officers among our passengers, and their claim would have precedence of mine though I might arrive at the post-station before them. So for a few hours I was content to stroll about the town—a few rambling rows of log-houses, surrounding a small market and a church, and extending for about two miles along the right bank of the Shilka River; and then, in the early afternoon, having purchased enough bread to last me for the next ten days, I made my way to the horse-station, and learned that a conveyance would be ready for me at six o'clock.

A few hours before sunset, on a fine calm evening,

with a tarantass and three horses, I set out from Stretensk on my journey of a thousand miles across the Trans-Baikal province to the lake from which it takes its name. I had a companion with me, a local Russian tradesman, who asked me to allow him to join me in hiring horses as far as Nertchinsk, the next town, but distant about a hundred miles.

Just outside the settlement we had to cross the Shilka by ferry-boat, and this was my first experience of a mode of ferry navigation which is common to all the great Siberian rivers. The motive power is simply the force of the current, which is made available for this purpose by a simple mechanical device. The big, ungainly, punt-like ferry-boat, on whose broad deck two or three tarantasses, each with a team of three horses, can be accommodated, is attached by a cable to a small boat-shaped buoy; by a second length of cable this buoy is attached to another; this also to a third; and so through a series of a dozen or more, until lying on the surface of the river is a chain of buoys and cables half a mile or more in length, the upper end of which is fixed by a strong anchor in the middle of the stream. When the ferry-boat is loosed from its moorings, the helm serves to keep it at such an angle to the current that it is carried by it over to the farther shore; by another turn of the helm, it is when required brought back again; and so, like a big horizontal pendulum, it swings to and fro from one side of the river to the other.

We were told at the next station that no horses could be supplied to us within eight or nine hours, and had it not been for my Russian travelling companion I should have had to stay there all night. But with his assistance I managed to hire, from a farm near the station, a team of three horses, and a light four-wheeled waggon called by the people a *telyega*.

One of the civilian passengers from our Amoor steamer had been waiting at this station with his wife and sister for several hours, whiling away the time by drinking vodka. When he saw me, with so little delay, mounting the cart to continue my journey, he was very angry; and having imbibed enough spirit to deprive him of his power of self-control, he stood on the doorstep and abused me roundly—being specially indignant, as he expressed repeatedly, that I, a fool of an Englishman, could actually travel along a Russian road, and with Russian horses, faster than he could himself.

A telyega is by no means an improvement on a tarantass. The wheels and shafts of both are similar, but the body of our telyega was simply a cradle of rough lattice-work, so shallow that our baggage more than filled it; and as we lay or sat on the top, there was not an inch of projecting timber, either at the back or on either side, to prevent us from falling off. The road was rough, the rolling prairie across which it ran being indented with numerous hollows, which the darkness converted into pitfalls. We went down with a sudden jerk into the smaller ones, and had several narrow escapes of being upset in the larger. The hours were the drowsy ones immediately before and after midnight, but as a moment's relaxation of our grip upon the ropes which bound our luggage to the cart meant an ugly fall, we were too much on the alert to sleep; and, for comfort and security, I don't think there is much to choose between the top of a telyega and the back of a buck-jumping horse.

The stage was an unusually long one of twenty-five miles. We did not pass a single habitation on the way, but a small village clustered round the post-station, which we reached between one and two in the morning. The village was in total darkness, and as still as death, when we approached, but the rattle of our waggon on the well-trodden street woke up a community of dogs, which began to bark ferociously. Our driver not being a regular post-horse yemschik, was not sure which house was the station, but, as locks are not much used in Siberian villages, every house was open to us.

The one we stopped at was a fairly large one, but with all its rooms on the ground floor. My Russian companion opened the door, and we went in together. We could hear no voice or sound; and except for the starlight through the windows, all was dark. Groping our way towards the interior of the dwelling, we found ourselves at length in a room, where evidently someone was sleeping. My companion, familiar with the customs of the country, did not seem at all disconcerted, and I tried to participate in his indifference; but our movements disturbed the sleeper; and whether that white figure which sprang up in bed, and asked us in such shrill tones who we were and what we wanted, was a man or woman, I do not know, for at that moment we heard the voice of our driver shouting to us from the street that we were in the wrong house, so we got out as quickly as we could, and found the post-horse station on the other side the road.

Horses were soon ready for us at this station, and, after the last few hours' experience of a telyega, a tarantass seemed a very comfortable vehicle. What sort of a road we had to travel on I never knew, for soon after we started I fell asleep, and I slept on until the familiar call of a cuckoo woke me, just in time to see the sunrise before our road dipped down into the valley, in which, on the banks of the river which gives to it its name, the city of Nertchinsk stands.

The little city of Nertchinsk was, up to the beginning of the present century, the eastern extremity of the Russian dominion. Until recent years it was the principal mart for trade with China, but most of this trade has now been transferred to Kiakhta—a town four hundred miles to the south-west, on the northern frontier of Mongolia. Nertchinsk again became notable for its proximity to the gold-mines and convict settlement of Kara. Most criminal exiles are now sent farther eastward to the island of Saghalien, but the lonely settlement of Kara still contains over a thousand prisoners, washing for the Government—from the alluvial river-bank—about 50,000 ounces of gold per year.

Nertchinsk is well situated on a steppe of the Lower Plateau, and about a mile from the Nertcha River; but it is an irregular, poorly-built, and unattractive-looking wooden city, with a population of not more than 4000, most of whom are engaged in cattle-breeding, and the cultivation of tobacco or cereals. A few merchants, trading in furs and brick-tea, also reside here, and the house of one of them — a palatial structure — is the only ornamental building in the place.

Before noon I was on my way again, but my progress was soon arrested; for, on reaching the banks of the Nertcha, we found such a strong wind blowing that the ferrymen refused to run the risk of taking us across, and we had to drive back to the city. After sundown, the wind abating somewhat, we made another start, and, though big waves were still breaking on the surface of the river, we succeeded in getting with our horses to the other side.

Through gorges in the Yablonovoi Mountains, which form the eastern border-ridge, we now began by gradual ascents to climb to the higher terrace of the Great Plateau. Most of the surrounding heights were thickly wooded, but some, with bare dome-shaped summits, rose above the others to an elevation of 8000 feet — beyond the tree-line in this latitude. The top of the plateau, 5000 feet above the sea, is wild and bleak, and farther northward is covered with perpetual snow. Its undulating prairie land is broken in some places by ranges of hills which rise from 1000 to 2000 feet above its surface, and are covered with forests of larch and fir and cedar, relieved by thickets of birch. The land between the hills is generally swampy and impassable; in other parts it is fertile, and affords good pasturage; but even in its most favoured spots, so exposed is its position and

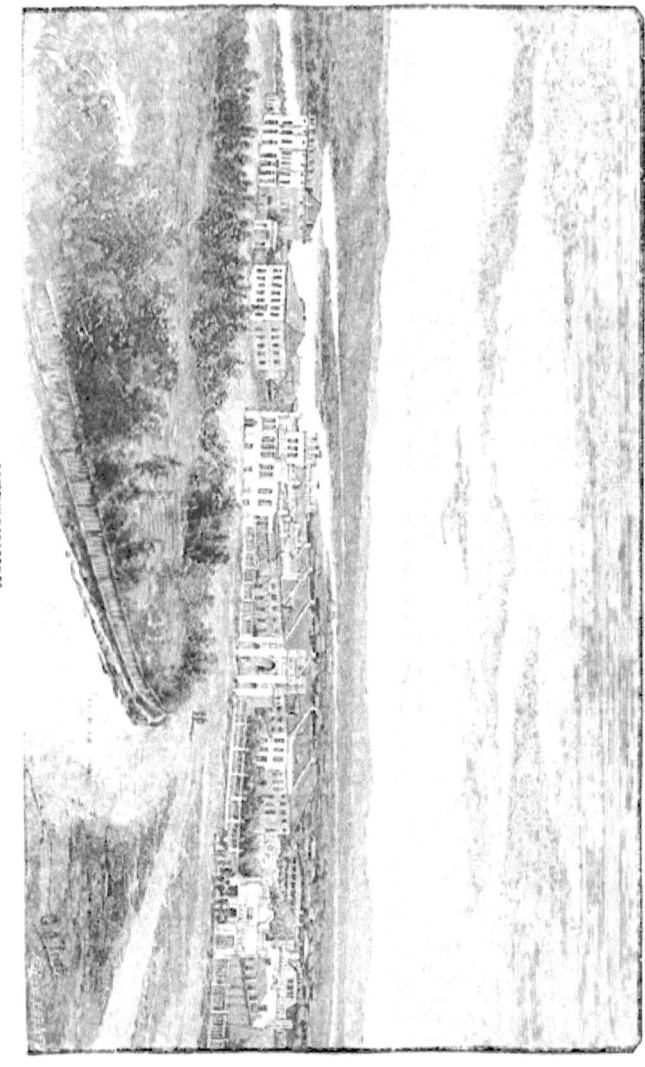

NERTCHINSK.

so short and uncertain is its summer, that agriculture is impossible.

In the daytime the cold did not seriously trouble us; the thermometer told us that the temperature was low, but the sight of sunshine was suggestive of the summer, and there was something in the going of these Russian horses which helped to warm one's blood. When warily picking their way through a broken bit of road, one shivered with the cold; but when the horses broke into their customary gallop, and with the jingling of bells, and the shouts of the yemschik, went up-hill and down-hill at their topmost speed, a thrill of sympathetic stimulation at once made the pulse beat faster, sent the tingling heat to the tips of one's fingers and the ends of one's toes, and, while the run lasted, made it easy to forget that the wintry air of the high Siberian table-land was round about us.

But we went on continuously night and day, only remaining at a station long enough to change horses and conveyance; and from sunset to dawn not only was the temperature lower, but there was nothing to divert our attention from it. One night there was a fall of sleet, which a strong wind drove fiercely in upon us. The wind was so cold he seemed to come direct from the North Pole, and so penetrating, that if there were the slightest chink or crevice in the arrangements of our rugs he was sure to find it, and then he put his icy finger through and touched one's arm or neck or leg — sending a shudder through our frame, and making us clutch desperately at the coverings to shut him out. But it generally happened that, in closing one aperture against him, we opened several others for his admission, and so we were driven to make another futile effort to exclude him; and thus through the cold night—with a few intervals of broken sleep—we managed to keep our blood in circulation.

After such a night, with joints almost dislocated by the jolting, and limbs almost frozen by the cold, it was cheering to look out in the early morning and see through an opening in the pine-forest the light of the sunrise on the neat white houses and churches of the city of Tchita. It was not so pleasant at mid-day to be trudging through its streets, over shoe-tops in sand; and still less pleasant in the evening, when a stiff breeze was blowing, to have that sand sweeping round one in clouds as dense as those of the sandstorms of the desert, or say, of other Siberian towns. And, welcome as this city is as a temporary oasis to the traveller, it must be rather a dreary spot to make one's permanent abode. Eastward and westward there is no other town within hundreds of miles; southward, at a considerable distance, are the waterless plains of Mongolia; and northward one might walk as far as the Polar seas without meeting any sign of human habitation. Yet there are twelve thousand people here, and the city is relatively important enough to be the capital of this extensive Trans-Baikal province.

Several thousands of the residents are soldiers, and a large proportion of the rest are in the employ of the Government. Not less than four thousand soldiers from Europe and Western Siberia pass through this city every year on their way eastward, and, as very few of them return, the Russian forces on the frontier must be accumulating fast.

The journey as far as Tchita is performed on foot, but the soldiers are sent on from here by raft, for, the Tchita River being a tributary of the Shilka—which forms, by its confluence with the Argun, the Amoor—there is a continuous water-way for rafts from this city to the Pacific coast. The rafts are broken up and their timbers sold on reaching the lower part of the Amoor, so that a fresh fleet is required every year. Some of the Government officials manage to make a good deal of money out of this raft-building; having them constructed less than the regulation size, and of slighter timbers, and then pocketing the balance of the contract price.

About two miles from the city, in a lonely spot on the banks of the Ingoda, enclosed by plain white wooden railing, I saw one day the grave of a former governor of this province, who, after embezzling large sums of money from the State by this raft-building, lost all that he had gained and more by gambling, and then came out here and shot himself. They buried him on the spot where he was found.

The climate of Tchita is peculiar. There is little rain in summer, and though there is a long ice-bound winter of over eight months, snow is as rare as rain; and, except on the rivers, wheeled vehicles take the place of sledges the whole year round. This scarcity of moisture is so seriously detrimental to agriculture, that the amount of grain produced is not sufficient for local requirements.

In the city of Tchita, and throughout this province, exiles are very numerous. Almost all the people engaged in menial employments — farm-labourers, herdsmen, and yemschiks — are ticket-of-leave convicts; and the Trans-Baikal is, in this respect, what Botany Bay and Van Diemen's Land were at the beginning of the century — a cesspool for the rascality and crime of the home provinces.

A dozen political offenders, exiled, not for any suspicion of a crime, but for sympathy with Socialism, are now located in Tchita. Though not allowed to leave the city, they move about freely within it, and in various kinds of skilled handicraft are earning their own living. They are in this way quite an acquisition to the town. If anyone wants a piece of ornamental furniture constructed, or a scientific instrument repaired, or has any work to be done which requires delicate and dexterous manipulation, he sends for one of these exiled Socialists. They do not visit among the people, though there is no wish to stand aloof from them, and they are often invited to social gatherings. Probably they attribute their exile to the reporting, by false friends, of some careless word spoken in such circumstances, and they do not mean to be caught in the same way again. The people here are very much surprised to find that men whose opinions are considered dreadful enough to merit exile are so well behaved; and the superintendent of the Tchita police remarked one day that if all the people here were as peaceable and law-abiding as these Socialists, there would be no work for him to do.

I met with an English lady in Tchita, the wife of a

TCHITA.

Russian physician who holds a Government appointment there, and it was an exquisite relief to the monotony of Siberian travel to spend an hour or two in their snug and hospitable home. The home was pervaded by the best of Christian influences, for the religion of the doctor and his wife was not of the superstitious Russian type, nor of that dreamy sort which begins and ends in heart-musings and soliloquies. They believed the faith of Christ to be indissolubly related to the progress and uplifting of the world, and so they were practical and warm-hearted philanthropists.

A few years ago the doctor visited America, and, after his return, his friend, Count Tolstoi, asked him what was the best new thing he had met with there? The doctor at once replied, "The Temperance movement."

To Tolstoi this idea was a revelation, but he eagerly embraced it, and set himself at once to organize the first Temperance Association in what is—with the possible exception of England—the most drunken country in the world.

A picnic had been arranged for that afternoon, and I was invited to join it. In the bright, warm sunshine we drove out to a narrow and secluded valley a few miles distant from the town. The deep, clear water of the Ingoda flowed with a strong current through it, and on either side rose rugged cliffs almost precipitously from the river. The rock was fissured and furrowed, and scooped out into caves and hollows and recesses, but evidently by no recent action of the elements, for the lichens had covered its surface with their hieroglyphics; every projecting ledge was fringed with fern-tufts; the mosses had woven a thick carpet at its feet; and the solemn pines which look down into the river from the top seemed to have stood on that brink so long they had lost all sense of danger.

The cliff-line in one place curves back abruptly to enclose between it and the river a broad green grass-plat; and here, as we lounged round the white tablecloth to our picnic entertainment; as we ate our English cakes and drank our English tea—or rather Russian tea in English fashion, with sugar and good cream; and as we talked in English—the first long English conversation I had had for weeks—of English friends and English homes, it was not easy to believe that I was in the very heart of the wildest province of Siberia.

Among my fellow-guests at this picnic was a prince. Datpak, or some such name, they called him, and he was a prince of the Tungus. It is well to meet a prince sometimes, if only to remind us how much like ordinary people princes are; and travelling in remote regions gives some of us the only opportunities we are ever likely to have of such interviews with royalty. The King of Tonga or of Timbuctoo is not so very unapproachable, and to meet him is to break at once the spell of a delusion to which perhaps we have been in bondage from our childhood. By right and birth and blood, as true a king as ever reigned; but having seen him once we henceforth know that our nationality is more important than our rank, and that more important even than our nationality is our kinship with the human race.

This Tungu prince had taken service in the Russian Army, and had been admitted to official rank. He was dressed in the military uniform of his promotion, and, having received a European education, was familiar with

TUNGU.

the conventionalisms of Russian social life; but in other respects he was a typical specimen of his race—of short stature, and slim but well-proportioned frame; with dark, widely-separated, and slightly slanting eyes; small but well-shaped nose; and squarish head covered with black hair.

Tchita seems to be the headquarters of the Tungus. They do not reside there, nor indeed anywhere else, for they are here to-day and gone to-morrow, being so persistently nomadic that they rarely remain forty-eight hours in the same place. Their houses are simply hollow cones of poles and reindeer-skins, set up in a few minutes, and as quickly taken down; and as they have no cumbrous furniture, this frequent change of residence involves little expenditure of time or effort beyond that of the journey from one place to the other. They come into Tchita to dispose of the furs which they have obtained in hunting; men and women riding into the city astride on reindeer.

Their clothing is made of the untanned skins of reindeer fawns; and both sexes dress so much alike, that, but for her veil and shorter stature, it would be hard to distinguish a woman from a man.

The vast forests of the High Plateau and of its eastern border-ridge are the favourite haunts of the Tungus, and the pursuit of game is almost their only occupation. The life of an agriculturalist or cattle-breeder is altogether too tame for them, and Prince Datpak was the only one of his tribe I heard of who had adopted European civilization.

They are evidently a Mongol race, and are probably the parent stock of the various tribes of aborigines— Goldis and Fish-skin Tartars—met with in the lower Amoor and Usuri regions. Some of the Tungus are reputed to be Christians; but though desultory efforts have been made to persuade them to submit to the rite of initiation to church membership, no pains have been taken to instruct them, and it is said that most of the supposed converts know nothing whatever of Christianity beyond the remembrance of the saint's name given to them in their baptism.

Their beliefs with regard to the Supreme Spirit and the future world are those of Shamanism, and either as the result of these beliefs, or in spite of them, the Tungus have attained a rectitude of life which has greatly impressed those who are best acquainted with them, and has placed them ethically far above all other Siberian tribes. Self-reliant and self-respecting, they will not brook an insult nor inflict one. Dishonesty is considered a disgrace, and thefts by them are said to be unknown. Courageous and persevering in the chase, they are able to enjoy and do full justice to a feast when they have been successful; but failure does not disturb their equanimity, and they can so patiently endure the pangs of hunger, that, after a day's laborious and useless effort, they will come back empty-handed to their empty wigwam, and, without a word of complaint, pull their waist-strap tighter, and lie down to sleep in the hope of better luck to-morrow.

Western settlers are encroaching more and more upon the hunting-ground of these people, and as they show no tendency to assimilate with their invaders, their numbers are steadily decreasing. The Government has tried to foster and protect them by special legislation, but so far these efforts appear to have been in vain. Races may, like men, be stricken with incurable decline; and this misfortune seems to have happened to the Tungus and their kindred tribes.

It is a stiff climb to the level of the Buriat steppe, one of the highest portions of the Great Plateau, and for more than an hour after leaving it Tchita was still in view. We had started at dawn on a fine calm morning, and when we reached the top of the ascent I turned to take a last look at the city. The mist which had been lying along the river had curiously gathered into a white dome-shaped cloud above the houses. Fires had been already kindled on many a hearth, and in the still air the chimneys sent up their lines of light-blue vapour directly to the cloud, which, with these filmy bands binding it to earth, seemed like a great white pavilion spread out over the city. A desert may be as safe to live in as a town, but, to the imagination, communities of men seem always to be canopied by some mysterious protective influence. We did not notice the pavilion while we were beneath it, but we missed its screening shadow when we went away. We had nearly four hundred miles to travel before reaching the next town, and as our horses turned over the ridge on to the steppe, whose grassy undulations spread before us like the sea, a thrill of lonesomeness, like a sudden fall of temperature, reminded us that the sheltering canopy was gone.

For scores of miles there was nothing to be seen except this rolling grass-land, which would have been an unbroken expanse of green but for the shallow pools which, here and there, reflected the blue sky. In some parts of the steppe we saw herds of horses and cattle grazing, and they relieved the solitude; their herdsmen were not visible, but we knew they could not be very far away. In other portions of the plateau, from one horse-station to another, there was no living creature to be seen.

Hills and forest-land at length appeared again on the horizon, and soon our road turned down into a broad open valley, where on the border of a wide mere lay a small village. We arrived there on the morning of Trinity Sunday, and all the people were dressed in their best clothes. But for this the village would have looked very dreary, for there was no paint on the houses, and nothing about them to relieve the dinginess of their old weather-beaten timbers. The land around them was trodden bare, and there was no such thing as a garden. It is a true instinct which leads the people of these villages to choose such warm, gay colours for their garments; and as on that Sunday morning the cottagers crowded to their doors to see us pass, the fantastic head-dresses and pink-flowered gowns of the women, and the red blouses of the men, did much to alleviate the otherwise universal sombreness.

But these Siberian peasants have other ways, less innocent than wearing their best clothes, of showing their appreciation of the fasts and festivals of Christianity. On Trinity Sunday evening, after the church services were over, the principal men and women of the village assembled in the travellers' room at the post-horse station, to honour the day by dancing and vodka drinking.

The piety of these people is peculiar. In the observance of Christian ceremonies they are most exemplary, and manifest for the externals of religion an almost superstitious reverence. Of those accounted orthodox among the poorer classes, few will enter or leave a room, or pass a church, or take anything to eat, without making the sign of a cross; and I have known the mere sight of a New Testament arrest a flow of bad language, and make a set of gamblers desist from play. But to many this reverential recognition of sacred objects is the sum-total of religion, and all that is believed essential for salvation is to admit the truth of the facts and traditions of the gospel, and to take part in the ceremonies which symbolise them. Of the spiritual meaning of those facts, and their bearing upon character and life, they seem to be unaware; and it never occurs to them that there is anything at all incongruous in showing their respect for the teachings of the Church by getting drunk.

The heaviest drinking is at Easter, which is perhaps the most popular religious festival in Russia. Whole villages then give themselves up for several days to wine-bibbing; and if an astonished stranger asks the meaning of such carousing, a chorus of voices instantly replies—and without the slightest intention of irreverence—"Why, because Christ has risen"; and at the word they chink their glasses and drink again.

There were similar scenes on Trinity Sunday; and, in some cases at least, the drinking was continued through the night, for passing through another village in the forenoon of the following day we saw a number of the revellers lying in drunken stupor about the road, and our yemschik had to turn his horses aside repeatedly to avoid running over them.

Having passed the steppe, we were among the trees again, and from the branches of one or more of them, on every little elevation near our track, strips of rag were fluttering. They had been placed there by the Buriats as charms against evil spirits. We were now in the heart of the Buriat country. The plain we had just crossed was called the Buriat steppe; Buriat yemschiks drove our horses; and at every post-station the Government notices had Buriat translations affixed to them.

The Buriats have characteristic Mongol features, but they are taller and more strongly built than the tribes met with farther east, and have much more energy of character. They maintained for many years an effective resistance to the Russian invasion, but the omens were against them: a great forest-fire destroyed over an extensive area the dusky pines, and white-barked birch-trees sprang up in their stead, and so the swarthy Mongols knew that they were destined to give place to the white-faced Russians.

But conquest does not to the Buriats mean destruction. Unlike the other tribes of aborigines, they have been able to adapt themselves to the new circumstances, and, side by side with the Russians, seem likely to hold their own. A few of them are engaged in hunting and fishing, but large numbers have become agriculturalists, and tens of thousands of acres in this province are cultivated by Buriat farmers.

producing abundant crops of wheat, rye, spring corn, and oats.

But by far the larger number of these people are employed in cattle-breeding. The herds we saw grazing on the Buriat steppe were Buriat property, and one individual sometimes owns as many as five hundred oxen and one thousand horses. They are good riders, and perform most of their journeys on horseback. We often met parties of them travelling in this way, the women sitting astride in the saddle like men. But this fashion of riding is not peculiar to Buriat women; many of the Russians have adopted it, and, judging from the number of officers' wives and other gentlewomen we saw taking horseback exercise in the neighbourhood of the settlements, the side-saddle appears to be quite discarded by the European equestriennes of Siberia.

The dress of the Buriats resembles that of the Russian peasantry; but the hair is cut short except on the crown, where it is allowed to grow to its full length and is formed into a pig-tail—much smaller, however, and more like a genuine pig-tail than the long, heavy plait of the Chinese. Women dress their hair into four pig-tails, and in married women these are coiled round a carved piece of wood about a foot in length, which lies across the back of the neck—a symbol of the marriage yoke. The pig-tails of girls not yet betrothed are, for the information and encouragement of wife-seeking young men, allowed to hang freely over the shoulders.

The religion of most of the Buriats is the Thibetan

form of Buddhism, but even among these the superstitions of their ancestral Shamanism are by no means extinct, as the bunches of torn rags which we saw hanging from the trees beside our road so plainly prove. The spread of Buddhism among them is comparatively recent, and has been fostered by the Russians; but efforts are now being made to convert them to Christianity, and, from a long conversation I had with a Russian priest who is engaged in mission work among them, I gather that the enterprise has met with encouraging success. If less easily persuaded to submit to baptism than other native tribes, they are far more staunch and thorough in their adherence to the faith when once they have accepted it; and Buriat members of the Church, who number now about ten thousand, are perhaps, next to the Russians, the only genuine Christians in Siberia.

They speak a language similar to that which prevails throughout Mongolia; but for their letters, which resemble Syriac though written vertically like Chinese, they are indebted to the Nestorian missionaries, who made such noble and self-sacrificing efforts to evangelise Far Eastern Asia a thousand years ago. Most of the books in circulation among the Buriats appear to be translations from Thibetan.

The Russian settlers in this province, though far superior to their Mongol neighbours, associate freely with them; and at one of the post-stations a Buriat offered himself to me as travelling companion. It is such a common thing for Siberian travellers to lighten the expenses of their journey in this way that a special word is used to describe these post-road partnerships; and when one traveller speaks of another as his *popootchik*, he simply means that the person referred to is sharing the expenses of his horse and carriage hire.

Though I did not accept the offer of the Buriat, in one part or another of my journey I had a number of popootchiks. Some of them were homely, honest Russians, who not only made my travelling cheaper, but pleasanter and more expeditious. Others did directly the reverse. One man showed his appreciation of my company by borrowing from me, to meet some pretended temporary emergency, a sum of money large enough to leave me stranded in the middle of Siberia. When he reached his destination he vanished like a ghost, and I had to get upon his trail, track him from one part to another of the settlement, and corner him at last, before he showed any disposition to refund.

But the worst of my popootchiks was one who joined me at a station on the other side of the Buriat steppe. He was a tall, big-boned, dark-complexioned man of about forty years of age, with some such name as Bruffski. He wished to share with me the expense of horse-hire as far as the next town, a distance of about three hundred miles, and with some misgivings I consented to the arrangement. We were to start at four next morning, but Bruffski did not turn up until six, and not only had he a bottle of vodka in his hand, but by the colour of his face and his demeanour it was evident that he had already a fair quantity of the same strong spirit in his head. As soon as we started he began to drink again, so I took the bottle from him and hid it in the straw; but he found and refilled it at the next station, and took care henceforth to keep it out of my reach. So drunk was he after the first day that he was seldom able to get into the tarantass or out of it without assistance.

He had a deep bass voice, and probably had been employed, at some time or other, as clerk of the responses in one of the Russian churches. He seldom spoke, but sometimes exercised his voice by sounding a long *oo* in a fairly deep tone, and then rolling it out an octave lower. The last *oo* generally resolved itself into a snore, and Bruffski lay beside me like a log.

But even the heavy stupor of intoxication could hardly render a man quite insensible to the erratic motion of a tarantass. In one place we were jerked about so violently that my cow-hide portmanteau was ripped open at the seams, and I had to gather its contents together at the next station in a blanket. That one's own skin remained unbroken in such circumstances is an unquestionable proof of its perfect toughness and elasticity.

But how the shaking jarred one's nerves! Bruffski had a big feather pillow at his back, but in his helpless drunken coma any unusual jerk made his head rattle against the side of the tarantass like an auctioneer's hammer on his block. At this he usually awoke, but only just long enough to shout, in stentorian voice, "Yemschik, stop!" And the Russian driver, accustomed to prompt obedience, at once pulled up his horses and stopped. But in less than a minute Bruffski was asleep again, and when I heard him snore I gave the signal to the yemschik to drive on.

And so we went on together all day and all night, and from day to day, the only compensation to me for the misery of such companionship being the thought that Bruffski was sharing the expenses of the journey. But even with regard to this some doubt at length arose. The man had, plausibly enough, suggested that, to save the trouble of dividing our expenses at every stage, it would be better for me to advance money for the first half of the journey, and let him do so for the second. But when my portion of the payments was completed, he coolly told me that he had no funds; so I had to continue my payments to the end, relying upon Bruffski's promise to refund his share of the expenses as soon as we reached the town.

Several days afterwards, late in the afternoon, we arrived at the little town of Verchni-Udinsk; and if I was glad to see it as the first town we had come to during the last four hundred miles, I was still gladder because here I was to part company with my drunken popootchik. My baggage was carried into the travellers' room, and Bruffski was surprised to see me take from my pocket a roll of rouble notes, thinking—as I had intended he should think—that I had only enough money with me to meet the actual expenses of the journey to this town. But for this opinion, and his own drunkenness, travelling with such a companion on dark nights and in lonely places might not have been particularly safe.

Bruffski soon went out and ordered another tarantass,

telling me that he was only going to his house in the next street, and that, if I would go with him, he would at once pay me what he owed. As we drove out of the stable-yard I heard my companion mutter to the yemschik, and I caught the words " out into the forest." Away we went at full-trot down one street after another till we reached the main road which leads out of the town, and I saw the fringe of the pine forest about half a mile ahead.

There were houses on either side of us, and people standing at the doors watching us, but in less than two minutes the last house would be passed, so I called upon the driver to pull up. Bruffski told him to drive on; and, as the horses were now going at a gallop, if I did not mean to be taken out into the forest against my will, it was evident that something must be quickly done. So, gripping with both hands Bruffski's pillow, I pulled it from behind him, and hurled it out into the road. At once he shouted, as I had so often heard him shout before when disturbed in his drunken sleep, " Yemschik, stop!"

He told the yemschik to fetch the pillow, and tried to detain me while he did so, but I was too quick for him; and as people from the houses came running up to see what was the matter, Bruffski thought it was time to get away, so he drove off into the forest, leaving the pillow in the road as his sole contribution to the expenses of our journey.

They told me at the post-station that all the horses were engaged, so I had to wait at Verchni-Udinsk until the next day. I went into the travellers' room, but found that it had already other occupants—a cosy company of two, which the addition of a third would spoil. They were a young Russian officer and his wife; and if it be true that courting habits do not persist long after marriage, this must have been a newly-wedded pair. The lady was resting her head against the shoulder of her husband, whose arm was around her waist, and they were very affectionately holding each other's hand.

Facing away from the door, they could not see me enter, and, thinking how shocked they would be to know that they had been caught in this position, I stealthily stepped back into the stableyard. But it was very cold out there, and, after walking up and down for half an hour, I went back to the room. The young couple were still in the same position, but as there was no other room available, and I was cold and hungry, I coughed, to warn them of my presence. I coughed very gently, but if I had had a fit of whooping-cough I don't think it would have made any difference; for afterwards I whistled, and then walked boldly up to the window without producing the slightest symptom of confusion, or the slightest change of attitude, either in the wooer or the wooed.

Others came into the room presently, both men and women, but, being Russians, they neither laughed nor frowned nor looked surprised, and it was evidently only to the Englishman that the situation seemed in any way peculiar. In China a man may not walk out with his wife, nor appear with her in public, under any circumstances whatsoever. In England a man need not shun his wife's company in places of resort, but he must not give any public sign that he has any special affection for her. In Siberia public manners are not so restricted, and the people evidently think no more of a kiss or a caress between persons who are married or betrothed than they do of ordinary hand-shaking among friends.

Verchni-Udinsk is a cheerful-looking little town, with the Uda River bounding one side of it, and the pine forest every other. It has a population of about five thousand, whose white dwellings are overlooked by the towers of three or four churches. The streets are very wide, but they have no pavement of any kind, and making one's way along them is like walking on some sandy shore above the water-line. In this respect it is worse even than Tchita.

Around the market-square are some good general stores, and the bazaar building in the centre is partitioned into a number of little shops, where some of the exiled Jews, who form such a large proportion of the residents, sell furs and jewellery and other kinds of Siberian produce. In most of the towns of England there are shops which advertise the wares they have for sale by a painted representation of them on the signboard. This custom, which is very general in the towns of European Russia, is almost universal in Siberia, and is a great convenience in a country where so large a number of the people cannot read. The signboards form together a sort of pictorial epitome of the social life of the neighbourhood. Various articles of male and female dress, house furniture, saddles and harness, agricultural implements, cutlery and crockery-ware, carpenters' tools, packs of playing cards, writing-paper and envelopes, firearms, musical instruments, plates of cakes and French rolls, dishes of sausages and brawn, steaming samovars, bottles of frothing kwass, decanters of vodka, pestle and mortar and boxes of pills, coffins and crucifixes,—all these things, and many more, may be seen represented in full-sized painted pictures on the signboards of any important Siberian town; and a stranger, wishing to make purchases, has only to walk along the street until he sees the likeness of what he wants, and he knows at once where it may be obtained.

Having replenished my store of provisions, I was ready to start again. The road from Verchni-Udinsk to Baikal—a two days' journey—crosses part of the north-western border-ridge of the High Plateau—a romantic region of rolling table-land and forest-covered mountains, affording from their slopes far-reaching panoramas of fertile valleys and winding rivers, with horses and cattle on their banks, and here and there a lonely farmstead.

Most of the settlers in this region are *Raskolniks* or Nonconformists, and are descendants of the men who, in protest against the Patriarch Nikon's innovations, severed themselves from the national church; and who, a hundred years ago, flying from the persecuting wrath of Peter the Great, came to these remote valleys. They and their children have steadfastly maintained their religious independence, and preserved their purity of blood; for among the Raskolniks on the banks of the Uda and Selenga may be found to-day some of the noblest specimens of the Russian race.

Near the town a second road branched off from ours to the southward. It leads to Kiakhta, and is the direct route through Mongolia to Pekin. These two are the only roads in this province, and so the greater part of the Trans-Baikal region is inaccessible except to foot and horseback travellers.

It was a splendid morning when I set out from Verchni-Udinsk. Only the yemschik was with me; I had had enough of popootchiks, and was glad to be alone. The country looked extremely beautiful, for the winter had passed and summer had come. In Siberia there is no spring to speak of. As the sun gains strength he melts the ice and dissipates the fog, and then, as if the face of nature had been touched by some magic wand, verdure and flowers break forth from every inch of soil, and in a few weeks the landscape has something of tropical luxuriance. When I left Lake Khanka, only a month before, there was hardly a leaf or grass-blade to be seen, and now there was vegetation everywhere. The higher slopes were red with azalea flowers, and many of the shrubs and bushes in the foreground were masses of white or pinkish bloom. The roadside was lined with purple crocuses, filling the air with a fragrance like that of violets. Then we saw beds of yellow daffodil and white lilies, and, more rarely, isolated specimens of that beautiful red lily which is peculiar to this part of Siberia. One's eye passed from these to throngs of pearly-white anemones, parades of poppies, and acres of orange-coloured peony, until, fairly dazed, it was a relief to rest on a soft blue area of forget-me-nots.

For a long distance our course lay between the pine-clad hills which enclose the Selenga River. Through the dense shrubbery on its banks we caught glimpses of the flowing water long before the river itself came into full view. It is a stream of considerable size, and at this season was rising rapidly from the inrush of melted snow. But the rise of the river from this cause is soon over; a little later comes the melting of the subterranean ice, and the release of pent-up springs; the inflow which results from this lasts longer, and so swells the river that cargo-steamers are able to run from far above Verchni-Udinsk down to Baikal and Irkutsk.

We forded many of its tributaries, and among them were some ideal trout-streams—tumbling over stony ridges, racing down beds of pebble, resting for a while in deep dark pools, and then flashing out again among rocks and boulders on their way to the larger river. Though I call them trout-streams, I could not obtain reliable assurance that trout are found in them; but if they are not they ought to be, for they are just the kind of stream that trout and anglers love.

Towards evening, losing sight of the cultivated land, we entered upon a long stretch of dense and continuous forest, and, about sunset, arrived at a solitary post-station, over which, on a Government notice-board, I read—"To Moscow, 5496 versts. To Petersburg, 6100 versts."

SELENGA RIVER AND VALLEY.

With such a distance yet to travel there was no time for other rest than that which the tarantass afforded, and as soon as fresh horses could be yoked we were off again.

Our halt was just as brief at the next station, which we reached about five hours later. It stood quite alone in the depths of the forest, from which it was fenced off by a rough pine-log stockade. The night was starless, there were no lamps on our tarantass, and when, half an hour after midnight, we turned out of the glimmering candle-light of the stableyard into the impenetrable blackness of the forest, the sensation was not a pleasing one. Before me I could just see the shape of the fur-clad yemschik, and upward, on either side, the outline of the pine tops black against the sky. It must have been by these that the yemschik made out his way, for there was nothing to be seen below. Then it began to get colder, and hour by hour, as the night advanced, colder still; until, starting from my dozing dreams, I half expected to look out upon the Polar seas.

The day dawned at length—a cold, grey morning, with a sky overcast, and a keen wind blowing. The very pines looked ragged and forlorn, as if they too felt the sharpness of the wintry air. Suddenly the forest opened, and immediately in front of us lay the edge of the table-land. Beyond it there was nothing but a limitless expanse of hazy white, and it seemed as if we were driving off the world. But a nearer prospect showed that what lay before us was not so unsubstantial, for the white surface we looked down upon was not thin air, as it appeared, but a vast plain of ice, which stretched away beyond the reach of vision to right and left, and on before, seeming in the distance to be continuous with the sky. This, the yemschik told me, was Lake Baikal.

Now I knew the meaning of this sudden change of temperature. Yesterday driving through fragrant valleys, beautiful with flowers and warm with summer sunshine, in the darkness of the night we had passed into another zone. It was this great mass of frozen water which had chilled the air; and if in June the Baikal Valley is so cold, in winter, when the snow lies deep for months along its shores, and fills the surrounding glens and valleys, the climate must be terribly severe.

After a few hours, as we drove southward towards the post-station, the frozen portion of the lake was left behind, and we saw only a sheet of steel-bright water, broken by a few detached ice-masses slowly drifting before the southern breeze to join their predecessors in the north.

Baikal is a fresh-water lake, and is one of the most remarkable inland sheets of water in the world. Its surface is 1500 feet above the level of the sea; it is nearly a mile deep; its length is equal to that of England; and it covers an area of 12,430 square miles. The Selenga and Upper Angara, and a large number of mountain streams, flow into it; and the Lower Angara, its only outlet, carries off its surplus waters to the Yenesei. Except where these rivers join it, the lake is surrounded on every side by mountains; most of them are covered with dense forest, and one of the peaks which look upon its southern shore attains the height of 7000 feet above the sea.

A striking feature of Lake Baikal is its loneliness. Both its surface and its shores are almost an unbroken solitude. There is not a single town upon its banks, and its villages are few and small. A steamer crosses its southern portion once a week during the short summer, but there is little other navigation. And the lonesomeness of Baikal is not relieved like that of the ocean by roaring surf and rushing waves, for, though its surface is sometimes swept by terrific storms, and at a few miles distance from the shore there is generally a strong breeze blowing, the water at its margin is often too still to give a sound. But this region is liable to frequent subterranean convulsions— rumblings and quakings and even rendings of the earth; and the constant apprehension of these portents makes the stillness weird and painful. The early Russian settlers, looking out upon the surface of the lake from the gloom of the forest which overspreads its bordering mountains, were so impressed with the mystic silence of that vast solitude that they named it "the Holy Sea."

I was glad of an opportunity of warming myself, and getting a breakfast of bread and milk and eggs at the Mecooski post-station, for this was wintry weather, and I had been out in it all night. No steamer had yet crossed the lake this year, but, as the ice on the southern half had been broken up and driven northward by the wind, traffic might recommence at any time. As I could obtain no information more definite than this, I had to make up my mind to wait at the post-station until a steamer came.

The hut for the accommodation of travellers, with the stables and yemschiks' cottages, stood on a small promontory jutting out into the lake. The sloping hillside at the back was covered with virgin forest, consisting chiefly of dark-leaved pines and larches, which crowded close up to the station buildings. No other traveller was there when I arrived, but I was not left long alone. In the evening a couple of Turco-Tartars came, one of them being the man Aplin who was a fellow-passenger on the Amoor. Other travellers came on the morrow, and in a few days our waiting-room was full.

Some poorer travellers found lodging for themselves in the outbuildings. Among these was a typical Siberian peasant farmer returning from Blagovestchensk to the Volga, and whom I had met with before on the way. His hair, which was getting grey, was long, and parted in the middle, according to the custom of Russian peasantry. He wore a coarse frieze frock, gathered in at the waist with a girdle; and his trousers, of similar material, were tucked into a pair of top-boots.

His wife had died at his little farm on the Amoor; and, if he could himself manage to get on in Siberia without her, he did not think his three children could. All his relations were in Europe, so he sold out and set off with his family for the old home. He had a rough canvas-covered waggon of his own, for which he hired horses from station to station. He seldom came into the travellers' room, but often sent the children in to warm themselves. At night he prepared a comfortable bed for them in the waggon, he himself sleeping among the straw in one of the stable-lofts. The eldest child, a girl of thirteen, was delicately formed, refined in behaviour and appearance, but much too pensive for her age. She was doing her best to take her mother's place, not only in caring for her two younger brothers, but also in trying, timidly but anxiously, to relieve the sense of desolation which weighed upon her father's heart, and made him sit for hours, bareheaded, gazing with a sad abstracted look at Baikal, as if thinking of the now lost companion who was with him when he crossed the lake before.

The travellers' room was a fairly large one, being really two rooms made into one; but it was much too small for the number of people in it. Our fellow-guests comprised three women, half a dozen children, and as many men. One woman was travelling with her two little boys to Western Siberia. She was a tall, strong, resolute, but kindly-looking person, evidently well educated, and of good social position. Another younger woman had her husband with her and an infant child. The third woman in our party was the wife of a Siberian trader,—a most phlegmatic man,—and the couple were travelling together to Irkutsk.

Tarantass-riding seems to be specially trying to the weaker sex, and when first alighting at a post-station most of the women that I met were in no very amiable mood. In most cases a glass of tea and a cigarette did much to calm their irritated nerves and smooth their ruffled tempers; but our trader's wife was not so easily appeased.

"I have ordered the samovar for you," her husband said; "and here are the matches and some cigarettes."

"*Sobaka!*"—you dog—was all the thanks he got.

With no perceptible change of colour, and with no suspicion of tremor in his voice, he turned to me and said, "Shall we go for a walk?"

The poor woman's anger had time to cool while we were out, but it had not taken advantage of the opportunity; and when her husband asked her, "Is your headache better?" her only reply was the same uncomplimentary reference to himself. She could talk fluently enough to others, but, until a day had passed, she had for her beloved only that one expressive word, and he listened to it every time with the same imperturbable tranquillity.

These, with the Turco-Tartars, and a couple of hide merchants and myself, were the company which lived and slept in that one room during the weary days of waiting for a steamer. We each had our own provisions with us, but, as there were only two small tables, we had sometimes to wait inconveniently long for an opportunity to get a comfortable meal. At night we had only to select a place on the floor to spread our rugs and blankets, and then lie down to rest. But with so many sleepers in one small room, the windows and doors of which were always tightly closed, the atmosphere soon became oppressive, and it was a great relief at sunrise to go out into the crisp morning air. Most of my fellow-travellers were content with a

Siberian wash, and thus left more room for the eccentric Englishman, who, in spite of the almost paralysing cold, preferred a splash in the big basin of the lake.

After the first day we had perpetual sunshine, making it a pleasure to wander in the pine-woods or on the shore. The lake was clear as crystal, and, at a little distance from its margin, blue as sapphire; but if a crag of ice came drifting by, it broke up the sunbeams which fell upon it into their prismatic colours, and the skirts of its robe of light were spread out upon the water like a rainbow.

Fish in the lake were rising freely at a small grey fly, —very provoking, when with so much leisure there was no angling apparatus within reach. Baikal abounds in fish of many kinds. Salmon appear to be most plentiful, and thousands of pounds worth are caught and dried here every season. One curious fish, the comephorus, is found only in this lake. It is of small size, and of the codfish family, but has never been caught, and never even seen alive. But after an earthquake, or an unusually severe storm, large numbers of dead ones are washed ashore. They are, when found, of the loose texture and mucilaginous consistence which characterize fish living under the enormous pressure of great ocean depths, and so it is inferred that the comephorus haunts the profoundest recesses of the lake. When exposed to sunshine on the shore their substance rapidly evaporates, leaving only a thin strand of integument behind.

Seals, though not fish, are a fishy sort of animal, and Baikal is the only fresh-water lake in the world where they are found. They are met with in great numbers at the north end of the lake, and the Buriat and Russian hunters sometimes secure as many as a thousand seals in one season.

The few days of sunshine quite changed the climate of the Baikal Valley, and made a great difference in the appearance of the country. Willows, birches, and aspens were seen bursting into leaf; and on a moist spot of sheltered land, on the outskirts of the forest, I found some flowers—beds of marsh-marigold, cinquefoil, wood-strawberry, meadow-rue, violets, and forget-me-nots. I might have found other spots as beautiful if I could have stayed a few days longer, but just then I caught sight of a steamer making its way towards us across the lake, and I had to hurry to the post-station to inform the others, and to pack my things.

In a few hours we were all aboard, and long before sunset were on our way to the farther shore.

CHAPTER X

THROUGH IRKUTSK TO TOMSK, BY TARANTASS

I CANNOT say that I saw the western shore of Baikal, for it was midnight when we arrived, and so dark that I am not sure whether what loomed before us was a hillside forest or a thunder-cloud. Before

LAKE BAIKAL, AND STEAMER LANDING AT LEESTVANEESHNIA.

dawn I was far away from it, for the post-station at Leestvaneeshnia—the long name of the little port where our steamer stopped—was quite close to the mooring-place, and had such a good supply of horses and tarantasses that I was able to start at once; and so, by seven in the morning, the fifty miles of intervening table-land was crossed, and I was looking down from the western edge of it at the city of Irkutsk.

A traveller approaching from the west can only see it piecemeal as he passes through its streets, but from this point the whole city could be seen at once, and to one just emerging from the eastern solitudes the sight was an impressive one. The plains below were covered for several miles with the white buildings of the city, among which, overtopping all the rest, stood the towers of numerous churches, their crosses gleaming in the sunshine, their base hidden by the thick foliage of the trees which had clustered round them. The beautiful Angara River, a third of a mile in breadth, curved half-way round the city on its way from Baikal to the Yenesei. There were gardens on its banks, and most of the surrounding land was under cultivation. Other towns and cities of Eastern Siberia are important only because they happen to be situated in a sparsely-populated country, but Irkutsk is a city which would attract attention anywhere.

It is much older than the cities farther east, and occupies the site of a still older Buriat town—a dirty Mongol settlement, which has now given place to the broad streets, handsome shops, substantial business offices, commodious hotels, and neat, cosy dwellings of the present prosperous city.

Much of its commercial importance is due to its situation near the junction of the two main routes by

which tea is conveyed from China to European Russia—
the sea route from the Yangtse to the Amoor, and the land
route through Kalgan and Kiakhta. But the chief source
of its wealth is in the mineral treasures of its neighbourhood. The gold-mines on the Lena have long been, and
are still, very productive; and large fortunes have been
made there by Irkutsk settlers.

Much of the wealth thus acquired has been expended
on the improvement of the city, several of its citizens
having made munificent bequests for this purpose. It has
more than one good school, from which youths go direct
to the European universities; two large public gardens;
a well-kept museum; civil and military hospitals; and
several orphanages, one of these being specially provided
for the children of Siberian exiles. Such an institution,
like a silver lining to a cloud, helps to soften the rigorous
aspect of the great Alexandreffski prison in the suburbs of
the city, and which, though only a temporary halting-place,
sometimes contains as many as two thousand convicts
waiting to be drafted to the eastern mines.

Irkutsk is the residence of a governor-general; and of
an archbishop, whose new cathedral, not yet completed,
has cost upwards of a million roubles. The city is also a
fortified military post, and the seat of several learned and
philanthropic societies, notable among the latter being a
branch of the Imperial Society of St. Petersburg, whose
special object is the prevention of abuses in the administra-
tion of prison discipline.

I reached this city on Sunday morning, and before Monday

noon was on the road again, commencing another tarantass journey of a thousand miles to Tomsk. There is much more traffic on this part of the post-road, and it is better made than its continuation farther east; but in other respects, beyond the suburbs of Irkutsk, the features of both are very much the same. Towns are still hundreds

THE MUSEUM, IRKUTSK.

of miles apart, but villages are more numerous, and every fifteen or twenty miles there is a post-station.

A considerable portion of the first half of the way is an avenue cut through one of those immense tracts of virgin forest called by Russians the *taiga*. In a few days we were in the midst of it, and, except at the lonely post-stations, there was nothing but the beaten track to indicate that human beings had ever visited these wilds before. Everywhere around us was the forest. It dipped down into the valleys, and spread itself out over the hills; all day and all night, and on from day to day, away from the

IRKUTSK CATHEDRAL.

stations, there was nothing to be seen but these close-clustered pines and cedars, and the dense underwood which found shelter at their feet.

One of the most marked features of the forest in the daytime was the absence of all signs of animal life. In the open country ground-squirrels were numerous all along the road. They sat on their haunches watching our approach, and with something like defiance in their look, but as we drew nearer their courage failed, and with a sudden somersault they dived headforemost into their burrows. But the forest seemed forsaken. Even birds were seldom either seen or heard, and, with the exception of a few moths and butterflies, winged insects were just as rare. A month later the place would be all alive with them, and mosquitoes in overpowering swarms make the forest uninhabitable either for man or beast. It is when crossing rivers, and flying towards the treeless plains to escape from these tormentors, that reindeer fall such an easy prey to their more formidable enemies the Tungu and Orotchi hunters.

The forest was not as deserted as it seemed. Often at nightfall, as the odour of the pine-trees began to exhale into the air, and their shadows to gloom upon our path, I saw wild deer bound across the track from one part of the forest to another. And there were plenty of other animals as well, some of which we were particularly wishful not to meet. Tigers have never been seen west of Baikal, and rarely outside the Usuri region; but no unsettled part of the country is free from the ravages of bears. Travellers who have to camp out in the woods at night run the greatest risks from these animals. Even a ring of fire around their sleeping-place is not a reliable defence, for a hungry bear is cunning enough to know that, having first got dripping wet in a brook, he has only to roll over on the burning brands and extinguish them.

But the most numerous and destructive beasts of prey in Siberia are wolves. They commit great havoc among sheep, but with a sort of cannibal propensity prefer to all other food the flesh of a dog, and often succeed in snatching one from between the very knees of its master while travelling at full gallop in a sledge or tarantass.

In the winter, when scarcity of food drives them to desperation, they do not hesitate to attack men; but a well-mounted Cossack will boldly ride into a moderately-sized pack of them, and, though armed only with a knout, will use it to such purpose that the wolves fly howling to the woods. When pursuing a tarantass, the pack, if not too large, can be kept at bay by tying a garment to a cord and letting it trail behind the vehicle; the wolves shy at the mysterious object like a timid horse, and will not venture to run past it. But a Siberian priest, a few months before I was there, when driving out alone in the forest, was killed by a pack of wolves. The horse brought the cart into the village without a driver, and, a few hours later, the search party found not only the bones of a man, but quite near them the fresh remains of a wolf. In the cart also had been found a recently-discharged rifle; and so it was inferred that the priest, having shot one of the wolves pursuing him, and venturing to alight to secure its skin, the horse had bolted, leaving his master defenceless to the returning pack.

At night the cold compelled me to keep well under my rugs and blankets, but sometimes I ventured to look out; and if those black things which I saw beside the road were not what they looked like—wolves, but only what the driver said they were—burnt stumps of trees, I cannot say that I ever saw a wolf in Siberia.

But I had once a chance of doing so. I had been talking about these animals, and that evening, a little after sunset, the yemschik suddenly pulled up in a dark corner of the forest and said, " Would you like to see some ? "

" Where ? " I inquired with some eagerness.

" Well," said he, " if you will just walk straight down into the forest there, while I stay here with the horses, I'll bet my bear-skin cap that before you have gone half a verst you'll see some wolves."

I did not go. The situation was one in which I appreciated company, and, if it were only a Russian yemschik, it seemed better to have him near.

Apart altogether from the wolves, the sensation of being alone in a Siberian forest, especially at night, has a flavour of its own. I had already had a taste of it in the Trans-Baikal region. The night was calm and clear, but the noonday sunshine could hardly have dispelled the gloom of that hollow in the woods. It may be that spots as dark, and to all appearance as secluded, are to be found in England, and even in the neighbourhood of busy towns; but it was not easy to believe it at the time, for imagination insisted upon looking at the actual scene in its relationship to the untraversed wilds around it, and the long interval between it and the nearest human dwelling. It was this which made the situation weird, and quickened one's inner senses into such unwonted acuteness and activity.

The fir-trees, for ever brooding over some great secret, made morose companions; but theirs was not the only presence. The Orotchis, in addition to the supreme god Anduri, and the gods of the earth and sea, believe in another spirit which haunts the deep forest shades. They call him Shahka, and, whenever they pass a spot like this, seek to propitiate his favour. It was not hard for me that night to understand the feeling which led the Orotchis to their belief. The very air seemed to palpitate with supernatural life; and, with no chirp of bird or hum of insect to disturb the silence, one could almost hear the music of the spheres; the tread of spirits on the vault of heaven; the heart-throb of the universe; and it was a positive relief when a crash among the shadows recalled one's thoughts to material concerns, as some bear plunged through the saplings, or some decayed giant of the forest fell.

Sometimes, and more frequently after we passed Irkutsk, we met other travellers going eastward—military men or emigrants; and at other times we overtook caravans, of perhaps a hundred or more carts, carrying tea to Europe. Almost every caravan we met going eastward was a caravan of big-wheeled barrels, in which vodka, the favourite strong drink of the Russians, was being conveyed from Western Siberia to remote settlements.

Occasionally when we thought we were alone we were startled by a sudden clank of chains, and, coming round a bend in the forest road, we met a gang of exiles on their way to the prisons of Kara or Saghalien. There were seldom less than two hundred persons in a gang—women as well as men. They wore long coats of coarse, earth-coloured frieze, and were chained together as they walked. A file of soldiers with fixed bayonets marched on either side; there were vehicles in front for those who were sick, and for the little children of the exiles; and so, beneath the shadow of the pines, without a word, and with no sound but the confused tramp of feet, and the mournful clanking of the chains, the procession wended its way eastward, never to return.

Exiles were first sent to Siberia in 1591, and for the last hundred years they have been going there in an almost continuous stream. It is said that from seventeen to twenty thousand are now sent out there every year; but this number includes many of the near relatives of convicts, who voluntarily go out into exile with them, and some who are banished for a few years only to the towns of Western Siberia.

The gangs of exiles we met on foot consisted entirely of criminals, and included amongst them some of the vilest of the human race. Capital punishment is extremely rare in Russia, and villains who in England would receive a death-sentence, and in some parts of the United States be lynched without judge or jury, are in this country sent out as exiles to Siberia. It is said, also, that Russian

A PARTY OF EXILES CROSSING THE YENISEI.

criminals are generally of a more hardened and desperate type than those of other European countries; and certainly, if the expression of their countenance may be taken as an index to their character, it is not easy to believe that there are any worse.

As in other similar companies of outlaws, we noticed many who appeared to have become criminals through the neglect or misuse of their faculties,—their moral malady was functional. But one look at others was enough to give the observer the impression that they were born for crime; that they evidently lacked some of the normal moral endowments of mankind; and ought, perhaps, to be classed with the maimed, the halt, and the blind. Congenital deficiencies and deformities had contributed largely to make them what they were,—their moral malady was organic.

The appearance of the women convicts shocked me most. If not actually worse than the men, they seemed so; perhaps because of the beautiful background of ideal womanhood against which their moral deformity was shown. Such faces I had never seen; some of them still haunt my memory,—deceit and malignity and other evil passions had traversed them so often, that they had trodden the features into a stony hardness from which 'nothing beautiful could grow.

A large proportion of these female prisoners were dissipated women, bloated with self-indulgence, and apparently dead to every consideration except that of personal profit and enjoyment. Others were evidently the prey

of influences more malign. One woman I noticed in the
gang walking along, in spite of fetters, with a defiant
air; with black, short-cropped hair, sun-bronzed countenance, high cheek-bones, lips as thin as paper, and
compressed so tightly one could hardly see that she
had a mouth at all, and eyes—with the very devil in
them.

At some distance behind her was another woman—a
different, but probably as desperate a character. Only
three or four and twenty years of age, her face of pink
and white was surrounded by a wealth of flaxen hair,
and she had such large, light-blue, dreamy eyes, it was a
puzzle for a while to tell whether the look in them was
one of childish innocence or precocious maturity of crime.
But on closer observation one was irresistibly reminded of
that sleek domestic animal which sits purring on your
knee, with paws as soft as velvet, and the most harmless-
looking creature in the world—until it sees a mouse, and
then how the tiger nature of the animal reveals itself as,
like a fiend incarnate, she tears the little wretch to pieces.
If this girl had been guilty of the crime charged against
her, these feline resemblances were true to life. But the
pity of it that the sweet angel-nature of a woman should
be brought so low!

There were many others there whose faces were
engraved with tragic histories, and one would have liked
to stop the gang to study them. But a glimpse had to
suffice, for the chains clanked to the pace of its advance
towards the next turn in the forest road, and in a few

minutes we were left to the companionship of the sombre pine-trees and our own more sombre thoughts.

But some of the gangs of exiles that we met were not on foot, but riding in little carts. They wore convict dress like the others, and so there was nothing in their appearance to indicate superior social position; but a glance at their faces was enough to prove to us that morally they were of a very different type: and I was not surprised to learn that these were not criminal, but political, exiles. I have referred already to some such in Tchita, and I met many others afterwards—men and women—in some cases of high character and blameless life, who, because within the circle of their acquaintance they have given expression to opinions which are considered to be unfavourable to the existing form of government, are sent out to spend the remainder of their lives in the desolate seclusion of some remote Siberian settlement.

There is no doubt that opinions subversive of social order and political stability are particularly rife in Russia, but the Government has yet to learn that its policy of severe repression is increasing the evil it wishes to destroy. It is illegal to give a public lecture in Russia, or to call together more than a very limited number of people for any private purpose whatever, even for a dinner-party in one's own house, without the special permission of the police, and, if such permission is granted, it is on the express understanding that detectives shall be admitted to the assembly. The intelligence of the Russian populace is increasing in vigour and activity, and thought cannot be much longer denied utterance. With a continually increasing pressure in the boiler, there is only one alternative; and if in Russian society the safety-valve of free discussion is to continue weighted thus with exile and Siberia, sooner or later the pent-up forces will release themselves by the explosive violence of revolution.

A large proportion of the exiles of Siberia are either political or religious; but in Russia the distinction between these two classes is not very clearly defined. The Russian Church is so closely connected with the State that dissent from it is a political offence, and the object for which religious Nonconformists are sent into exile is not so much to extirpate false doctrine as to uphold the power of the Government. It is said that there are not less than fifteen millions of Dissenters in European Russia, and this is evidence of a considerable degree of toleration. So long as a religious sect continues stationary, does not promulgate its doctrines, and only enlarges by the natural increase of its own families, it is generally free from molestation. But when, like the Stundists, a sect becomes aggressive, disseminating its opinions, and seeking to win outsiders to its fellowship, it comes at once into collision with the ruling powers; and any member of another church—whether Dissenting or Established—who joins it, puts himself thereby outside the law, and forfeits all claim upon the Government for the protection of either property or life. The only change of religious denomination allowed to a Russian subject is from one of the sects to the Imperial Church.

There is no attempt to extort a disavowal of heterodox

opinions, and the only semblance of a religious test imposed upon the people is the paying of tithes, and the attendance once a year at the parish church. If there is any narrowness about the clergy, it is rather ecclesiastical than moral. They have their stated round of duties, and they do not allow their calm performance of them to be disturbed by much zeal for righteousness, or love for the souls of men. They are very lenient to their parishioners. Habitual drunkenness, dishonesty, licentiousness, even atheism itself, if not too noisy, seldom provoke serious denunciation, and are regarded as venial offences compared with that of joining the Dissenters—a mortal sin, which no amount of intelligence, education, or saintliness can palliate. So long as a man can keep himself above the suspicion of such a crime as this, the priest will treat him most indulgently; and, if his tithes are regularly paid, even the annual attendance at church will not be rigorously enforced.

The priests of the Russian Church have some excuse for their lack of ethical enthusiasm in the restrictions imposed upon themselves. Their duties are rigidly prescribed, and there is little liberty allowed for spontaneous evangelical effort. They are not required to preach, and if they wish to do so they must first submit their sermon to the inspection of the clerk of the diocese. Even after it has been thus inspected, an unguarded sentence in its delivery may expose the preacher to degradation and imprisonment.

So far, the efforts of the Russian Government to enforce religious conformity have failed. The more Dissenters it sends out to Siberia, the more there are to send. Exclusion of the light has not so much prevented development as changed its character, and made what would have been otherwise a blessing a curse. In the darkness noxious moulds and fungi flourish, and even wholesome plants, if forced to grow there, are apt to assume grotesque shapes and ghastly colours, and acquire deleterious properties. So with independent religious thought in Russia: having been denied the light of day it has had to do its best to flourish in obscurity, and there is perhaps no other country in the world in which that thought has, in the name of Christianity, attained such preposterous developments.

Many of the Dissenting churches of Russia are of the Lutheran type, and share the beliefs of the most influential parts of Christendom. One modern sect resembles, in name at least, our Salvation Army, for its members call themselves "Soldiers of the Spirit." They are great colonizers, and are numerous in some parts of Siberia. Other small bodies of Christians there are, scattered about the country, which have also unmistakably among them the Life which was the light of men. But side by side with these are some of the strangest Christian sects in the world. Most of the dissent of Russia is characterized by a leaning towards the communistic teaching of the earliest days of Christianity, but in some cases it is avowedly seditious and anarchical. One sect refuses to recognise the State, regards the Czar as Antichrist, and allows no prayer for him. Another sect does not pray at all, teaching that all rites and ceremonies, including prayer, have been abolished by command of God. Another sect derives its name from its belief that it is wrong to pay taxes. Another openly advocates armed resistance to the civil and ecclesiastical authorities. Another sect obliges its members to associate only with one another, and refuses to hold any communication whatsoever with the wicked world. The sect of "the Denyers" holds that nothing sacred now exists on earth. Other sects are grossly immoral—some making marriage dissoluble at will; others prohibiting it altogether, and advocating free love. One sect enjoins self-mutilation; and another teaches that as God called upon Abraham to offer up his son, so He may call upon us to do the same,—and hundreds of children, fourteen years old or under, are said to have been put to death in this way.

The very idea of sending people into exile for their opinions, and especially for their religious opinions, naturally excites the indignation of all who have been taught to regard liberty of conscience as the inalienable right of man. But a careful study of the eccentricities of Russian religious life and teaching—so grotesque, so impracticable, and, in some cases, so subversive of all law and order and morality—would show us, perhaps, that the problem before us is by no means such a simple one as we supposed. Other powers might find for these evils a milder and more effectual remedy, but for a despotic Government like that of Russia the method of dealing with them, however unwise, could hardly at present be other than it is.

On my way through this and the adjoining provinces I not only met many companies of exiles, but sometimes stayed in the village where they halted for the night; and, apart from the question of their innocence or guilt, they had, as prisoners, little to complain of except the hardships inseparable from such a long and difficult journey. Criminals had to travel the whole distance between the Ural Mountains and the Amoor on foot; but they were never required to walk farther in a day than from one post-station to the next. Free emigrants often do the same; and so of course must the soldiers in charge of the gang. Political exiles, and such criminal exiles as are pronounced by the medical inspector too weak to walk, have horses and carts provided for them. Neither class of convicts travel more than three or four days without being allowed one for rest. At the stations where they halt, log-huts are provided for them, and they are supplied with two substantial meals a day, each of which includes beef or fish.

Arrived at their destination, criminal exiles are generally sent to work in some of the Government mines, but after about eight years of servitude, unless they have been guilty of some flagrant breach of prison discipline, they are set free, and permitted, under the surveillance of the police, to make a home for themselves in one of the neighbouring settlements. Those who are exiled for their opinions—whether political or religious—are never sent to the mines, but are located at once in one of the towns or cities of Siberia, being allowed to live in their own house and get their living as they choose.

Such are the Government regulations for the disposal of its exiles, and in the great majority of cases these regulations are faithfully observed. But complications may easily arise. It is not strange if an honourable man, sent into exile for his convictions, has his temper ruffled by a rankling sense of the injustice of his punishment, and if he is in some instances provoked thereby to resent and resist the indignities to which he is subjected. But such resistance is a crime, and renders its perpetrator liable to be transferred to the gang of felons on their way to penal servitude. And if anyone, of either class of exiles, has the misfortune to bring upon himself the ill-will of the officials near him, there are plenty of ways in which, outside the law, he may be made to suffer for it. However good may be the intentions of the Government at St. Petersburg, and however humane its laws, it cannot, in such a distant and unsettled country as Siberia, exercise efficient control over the executive; and as throughout the empire there is no free press, the exiles have little except the Christian honour of their overseers to protect them from the freaks of arbitrary power.

It is not, therefore, at all surprising that irregularities occur, but they do not appear to be as frequent as some suppose. In reading descriptions of prison life in Siberia, we often commiserate as hardships deprivations which belong to the ordinary lot of Russian and Siberian peasantry. And the actual instances of cruelty and oppression which are from time to time reported, and which, justly enough, fill us with horror and indignation, are breaches of the law which the Government has neither sanctioned nor approved. They are to be classed with the similar outrages which in former times not infrequently occurred at our own convict stations in Australia, and with the lynchings which are so common to-day in some parts of the United States.

The convict stations of the Trans-Baikal province resemble in many respects ordinary Siberian villages; there is no insurmountable surrounding wall, and it is by no means difficult for an exile to run away. But more effective than artificial barriers is the broad area of wild, inhospitable forest which on every side surrounds the settlement. No one ever thinks of attempting to escape in the winter, nor when winter is approaching, but the spring seems to offer a favourable opportunity. The cuckoo is always heard in his season in Siberia. The exiles speak of him as "the king of the woods"; and when, after the long winter, his first familiar call is heard, the prisoners say among themselves, "The king of the woods is calling, it is time to get away."

Every year a considerable number respond to the cuckoo's invitation. The watch is not particularly close, and they need not wait long for an opportunity to slip away unobserved into the forest. But most of them soon find that flight does not mean freedom. Once, on an ocean steamer, a thousand miles from land, some ducks whose pen had been carelessly left open flew overboard. When last I saw them they were flapping their wings, and scuttling about on the water, in high glee at their escape. Before night, if a shark had not already snapped them up, they were no doubt bitterly regretting that they had left the ship. Such liberty as the ocean gave those ducks, the forest gives the exile. He may in the autumn sustain life for a time with berries and cedar-nuts, but nothing edible is ripe until the end of summer. The wilds around him are infested by beasts of prey; the nights are bitterly cold; and he has no place of shelter. He must not show himself in any village nor at any house, for his passport would be at once demanded, and he has none to show. He dare not even meet a fellow-man, except to overpower and kill him; and it is only by some such desperate deed that he can preserve his own liberty and life. Plunging into the depths of the forest, a month of continuous plodding will hardly be sufficient to bring him out upon the other side, and, apart from the other risks of such a journey, he finds himself at the very outset perishing with cold and hunger. So formidable are the difficulties which confront these fugitive exiles, that, of all those who escape from the convict stations, one third come back and ask to be readmitted, and one third perish in the forest, the remaining third only managing to maintain themselves in freedom.

These escaped exiles—called by the settlers *bradyaga* or *varnaks*—are the terror of the Trans-Baikal province. They are said to number not less than twenty thousand. One by one, as they manage to obtain passports, they set out for Europe, keeping well hidden by the forest while following the direction of the post-road. Most are content to run the risk of travelling with forged papers. An escaped exile who is determined to have a genuine passport must murder, rob, and personate a man who has one. Such a varnak is to be feared. He cannot procure firearms, but has taken care to bring a knife with him from the prison, and that suffices for his work. Taking his stand beside the forest road, in the morning or evening twilight, he awaits his opportunity, and then springs into a tarantass upon some solitary sleeping traveller, cuts his throat, appropriates his papers, hides his body in the forest, and bribing the driver—who is probably himself an exile—to secrecy, he continues his journey with the post-horses in the dead man's name.

I passed a lonely cottage in which, only a day or two before, a peasant and his wife had been murdered for the sake of their passports by one of these varnaks. Every traveller I met in that region was armed; and one who for a few hundred miles shared my tarantass, always sat for an hour or two at twilight, revolver in hand, looking down at the road from his side of the conveyance. He insisted upon me doing the same on my side, giving only one direction simple and precise: "Any man who shows himself here is a bradyaga, so shoot him without a word."

Happily, while this bloodthirsty companion was with me, we met no one; but one day when travelling alone through a wild part of the Trans-Baikal country, at about three o'clock in the morning, I awoke with a start. The sky was grey with the early dawn; the yemschik was nodding half-asleep on his box; the horses were pacing lazily along the track; and stepping out towards me from the forest, only a dozen yards away, was as desperate a looking villain as any convict gang could show. He abruptly stopped at the first sight of me, and, seeing that I was prepared for him, slunk back into the forest and disappeared.

What it was that aroused me at that moment into such alert wakefulness must, like many similar experiences in men's lives, be left as an enigma,—unless what Dibdin's ballad says of sailors is true also of others, and that travellers by land have some sleepless unseen attendant, like

> "The sweet little cherub that sits up aloft,
> To keep watch for the life of poor Jack."

But what Russian travellers from the East to Europe were that year specially afraid of was, not the knife of the assassin, but the pestilence that walketh in darkness; for the rumour had spread abroad that cholera had broken out again in Tobolsk and Tomsk, and the post-road crossed the infected region. Central and Eastern Siberia, except on the coast of the Pacific, are free from epidemics; and, rigorous as is the climate, it is one of the healthiest in the world. Some of the doctors holding Government appointments there complain that they are in danger of forgetting all the practical part of their profession, they have so little to do. The air on the Great Plateau appears to be too cold and pure and dry for the germs of tubercle; and I did not see a single case of pulmonary consumption, nor even hear of one, throughout the Amoor and Trans-Baikal provinces.

Acute inflammation of the lungs is perhaps the commonest serious disease, but it either kills its victim outright in a few days, or leaves him with his breathing apparatus unimpaired. Valvular diseases of the heart also occur here, and generally run a rapid course. Owing to the large amount of salt fish which enters into their winter dietary, scurvy sometimes appears among the peasantry; and diseases due to an immoral life are not only found among the Russian settlers, but have been communicated by them to the aborigines.

Considering the amount of talk which has been rife in England on the subject of Siberian leprosy, I was surprised to find it such an extremely rare disease. I inquired for it everywhere from Vladivostock to the Ural Mountains, but the very name for it was unfamiliar to ordinary people, and I did not meet with a single leper from one end of the country to the other. There is a small leper settlement among the Yakuts on the Lena, and another near the coast, but all the lepers in the country, according to the carefully-prepared Government register, number less than seventy. Being so few, they are well provided for; and the poorest of them owns a cow and a plot of land.

It was stated in the English newspapers, a few years ago, that somewhere in Siberia an herb had been discovered which was a specific for this terrible disease, and a successful appeal was made for subscriptions to send a costly expedition to the Lena to ascertain what this herb might be. The price of a few postage stamps, and a letter to any respectable Russian physician, would have elicited the information that the herb referred to was the well-known sarsaparilla, that it had unaccountably acquired a temporary reputation as a cure for leprosy, but that, after zealously administering it for a considerable length of time to every known victim of this disease in Siberia, with no improvement whatsoever, the employment of this herb in the treatment of leprosy had been abandoned.

It was probably because of the general immunity from epidemic diseases enjoyed by Eastern Siberia that the rumours of cholera in the West created such alarm. Several of my fellow-passengers on the Amoor steamer were so disturbed by the reports received, that they gave up the journey, and postponed their return to Europe to another year. The prompt and vigorous measures adopted by the Central Government to cure, if not prevent, the malady, increased the panic of the people. No attempt was made to warn them against the danger of drinking contaminated water, and filters in Siberia are unknown. If I asked for water, they never brought me any that it was safe to drink. Sometimes it was green, and sometimes brown, and always tainted with decayed organic matter. But, as the average Siberian peasant only uses water to dilute his vodka and infuse his tea, the danger may have been less serious than it seemed.

There was no stint in the supply of disinfectants, and around every post-station between Irkutsk and Tomsk there was always a strong odour of carbolic acid. Every sniff of it awakened gloomy apprehensions in the people; but what disquieted them most was the rough wooden shed which, by Imperial order, had been erected on the outskirts of every town and village as a hospital for those who might be stricken with the disease. Its isolated position, and the new white deal boards of which it was constructed, made it a conspicuous object; but, in passing the first one I had seen, it was necessary to ask the yemschik what it was, and putting his hand to his mouth, with awe in his look, he whispered in my ear—as if afraid to hear his own voice utter it—the one word, "Cholera."

The dread of this mysterious enemy produced a strange effect upon the superstitious imagination of the people. In some parts of the country they personified the evil, expecting to see it walk into the settlement in human form; and on one occasion, a stranger, who appeared suddenly in a village, was declared to be the cholera. The villagers at once seized him, and he was only saved from a violent death by the timely arrival of his friends.

Towards the middle of this portion of the journey I sometimes found it convenient to hire outside horses. They were cheaper than those supplied at the post-station, and quite as good. Many of the farmers were able to supply us, and some of them were so anxious to earn money in this way, that they often rode out several miles from the settlement to meet in-coming travellers, and strike a bargain with them for the ensuing stage. The disadvantage to the traveller was that tarantasses could only be obtained at the post-station, and if he went elsewhere for horses he had to be content with a telyega—one of the shallow, open waggons already described. Such a conveyance is bad enough in the daytime, but is almost unendurable at night, for, however carefully the baggage is arranged, it is impossible to find a position in which we can sleep securely, and we have to be thankful for a few minutes of semi-conscious dozing when the road happens to be smooth.

To make matters worse, there was one night a continual fall of drizzling rain, which, an hour or two before dawn, culminated in a violent thunderstorm. It burst upon us suddenly—a few premonitory rumbles, and then the din of universal battle, as the thunder, peal after peal, crashed and roared and echoed through the forest, while, the dome of darkness round about us riven by the concussion, the gleaming fissures here and there ran down its ebon walls, only to be instantly repaired.

We were in a fine position to see it all, perched on the top of a pile of baggage, with only the sky above us, and the wild taiga around. And we had to see it to the end, for neither coaxing nor imprecation nor any amount of whip could make our horses face the rain and sleet which the wind was now sweeping furiously along our course. At first there was a sense of danger and of loneliness, but soon the impressiveness of the phenomena made us forget all else—until, drenched to the skin with the cold rain, we became conscious only of intolerable discomfort; and then, at last, in our despair we too caught the defiant mood of nature, and told the contending elements to do their worst, we did not care.

Four hours later we emerged from the chaos of the storm, and of the forest, to see before us on the plain a settler's homestead, and no palace parlour can appear more cozy to a king than did that well-warmed hut to me; nor can the daintiest dishes at a banquet be more inviting than was that basin of hot bread and milk.

When we drove forth again, the winds were hushed and the birds were singing. Before us lay the flowery beauty of the steppe; above us was the calm blue sky; around us everywhere the genial warmth and golden glory of the sunshine; within one short hour pandemonium had been transformed to paradise—"so soon a smile of God can change the world."

We had only passed two small towns, Nijni-Udinsk and Kansk, in the six hundred miles we had already travelled from Irkutsk, but we had not gone far this morning over the undulating plain when we found it suddenly sloping down into a deep broad valley, so broad that the high lands on the other side of it appeared only like a sinuous purple line on the horizon. This was the valley of the Yenisei; but the great river keeps so close to the western border that we could hardly see it at this distance, and could only be sure of its position by the city of Krasnoiarsk, which stands upon its banks, and whose white church towers, illuminated by the sunshine, were distinctly visible some twenty miles ahead. We reached the river in a couple of hours, the yemschik driving down into the valley at such a furious pace that when one of our horses fell the two others dragged him along for at least a hundred yards before we could bring them to a stand.

The eastern bank of the Yenisei was quite busy that day with a traffic representing very adverse interests. Old topers would have been filled with a hankering desire at the sight of a caravan which had just crossed the river—a caravan of vodka, great hogsheads on wheels, conveying to the settlements of Eastern Siberia the strong rye-spirit of which Russians are so fond, and which so ill repays their fondness. Members of temperance societies would have been delighted to see there, waiting to cross over, a caravan of nearly a hundred cart-loads of tea on its way from China to Europe. Those who were too whimsical to look with any favour upon tea might yet find satisfaction in thinking of that simpler beverage, of which they had such an inexhaustible supply in the clear cold water of the river.

This river is the largest in Asia, and one of the five or six largest in the world. Rising, on the table-lands of Mongolia, 5000 feet above the level of the sea, before it reaches that level it must run a course of more than 3000 miles. At the spot where I crossed it, more than 2000 above its entrance to the Arctic Ocean, it is half a mile wide; and it is navigable for several hundred miles above this place, steamers running regularly in the open season as far as Minusinsk, on the frontier of the Chinese Empire. We crossed the river with our horses on a sort of raft —a large platform supported on three parallel boats, and which was swung over to the other side by the force of the current acting on the pendulum arrangement already described.

The province through which this river runs is named from it Yeniseisk. The vastness of Siberia may be inferred from the fact that this one province is more than half as large as European Russia. Krasnoiarsk is situated on the western bank of the river; has a population of fifteen thousand; and, though not the capital, is the largest and most important city in the province. It is well supplied with churches, and their tall painted towers serve as landmarks for long distances away on the bordering steppes. The city is well laid out, its streets are straight and wide, and it has a considerable number of substantial brick buildings—residences, offices, and shops. One of the latter is known as "The English Store," a name which irresistibly attracted me to visit it; but none of the people about it now are English, and its present claim to the title of "English Store" rests only on the stock of Birmingham hardware it has for sale. But the business was established by an Englishman, and until quite recently was in his charge. He was greatly interested in the efforts made to open direct sea-traffic

KRASNOIARSK CATHEDRAL.

between England and Siberia, and when the enterprising English captain, who has been the pioneer of this service, arrived in the Yenisei off Krasnoiarsk, the owner of the "English Store" at once set out for the ship to offer his congratulations, but his boat capsized and he was drowned.

Glass and soap and pottery-ware are manufactured here, and there are some large tanneries; but the prosperity of the city and its neighbourhood depends mainly on the mines of the Yeniseisk taiga — the best-paying gold-fields of Siberia.

It is intensely cold here in the winter, and the low temperature is made more trying by the strong winds which then prevail. In one way these winds are very serviceable—they keep the streets clear of snow, sweeping it away as fast as it falls; but they cannot melt the ice, and the river remains frozen over for about half the year.

A hundred miles west of the Yenisei we crossed the Tcholym. At certain seasons of the year this river, which is a tributary of the Obi, is navigable for several hundred miles, and affords a good water-way to Tomsk; but I arrived too early in the year for this mode of travel, and so had to continue my journey with horses as before.

The little town of Atchinsk, where the post-road meets the Tcholym, is the centre of one of the principal horse-breeding districts of Siberia, and these animals are so plentiful and cheap that the charge for hiring them at the Government post-stations is only half what it is at the stations farther east. At one village, where the stables of the post-station happened to be empty, to save delay we hired from a farmer a team of three horses and a telyega for the next stage of about twenty English miles, and the total charge for horses, vehicle, and driver was one rouble—or two shillings in English money.

A good horse—equal to the best at the post-stations—could be purchased for £3 sterling. Cattle were equally abundant. The average price of a milch cow was £1, and I have seen calves a few weeks old sold for 1s. 6d. each. There are few other civilized countries in the world where all the necessaries of life can be obtained so cheaply as here. Ten pounds of Russian bread could be purchased for 2½d., a pound of beef or mutton for 1d., a hundred cucumbers for 2d., thirty-six pounds of potatoes for 2½d., a fowl for 1½d., a duck for 2½d., and a goose for 6d. Fresh eggs were regularly sold at five or six for 1d., and new milk at a halfpenny per quart. Most of the settlers build their own houses, but anyone wishing to rent a substantial little log cottage in one of the villages could do so for about £1 sterling per year.

This is a poor district for earning money, though such a good one for economically spending it. The population is not nearly so sparse as in the Amoor and Trans-Baikal regions; and though the soil is fertile, and a small fraction of it suffices for local requirements, it is impossible, in the absence of cheap and rapid means of transit, to find a market for the surplus produce. The establishment of regular steam communication between the Yenisei and Obi Rivers, and the chief ports of Europe would greatly enrich this district, and at the same time confer benefit upon the dense populations of Western Europe, by placing a larger wheat supply at their disposal, and opening new markets for their manufactures.

A considerable proportion of the present population of this part of Siberia are Tartars. Except in the large towns they do not mingle with the Russian settlers, but have their own separate villages, which are distinguished by a special style of building, and a central mosque, which looks so much like a church, that I had seen a considerable number of them before I noticed that the gilded object surmounting the tower was a crescent and not a cross.

The word Tartar — or, more correctly, Tata — was originally the special designation of a Mongol tribe in the desert of Gobi, but was thence adopted by the people of the West as a convenient term to describe the composite hordes of Turks and Mongols which devastated Eastern Europe six centuries ago. The Manchurian race which now rules the Chinese Empire is often spoken of in the West as Tartar; but, as generally understood to-day, the Tartars are a Turkish people mixed in various degrees with some of the aboriginal races of Finland and Mongolia. They have crossed the Ural Mountains, and formed large settlements in European Russia; Kazan, on the Volga, is a Tartar city, but Siberia is their native land. From the banks of the Lena, where they were first heard of, and where they still have the important township of Yakutsk, they have spread over a considerable area of the province of Yeniseisk and the governments of Tomsk and Tobolsk. Most of them are engaged in cattle-breeding and agriculture, but some of them travel about the country buying and selling various kinds of merchandise, and some are employed as artisans in the larger towns.

The Tartars living on the Lena, and in the neighbourhood of Minusinsk on the Upper Yenisei, are at least nominally Christian; but the great majority of the Tartars of Siberia are Mohammedans. They are faithful to the

TARTAR OR TATA.

outward observances of their religion, dropping down on their knees to pray at the appointed times, wherever they may be, and in whatever company; but it is to be feared that in most cases their religion ends with these observances, which are valued not so much as a means of virtue as its substitute.

The Tartar men are moderately tall, broad-shouldered,

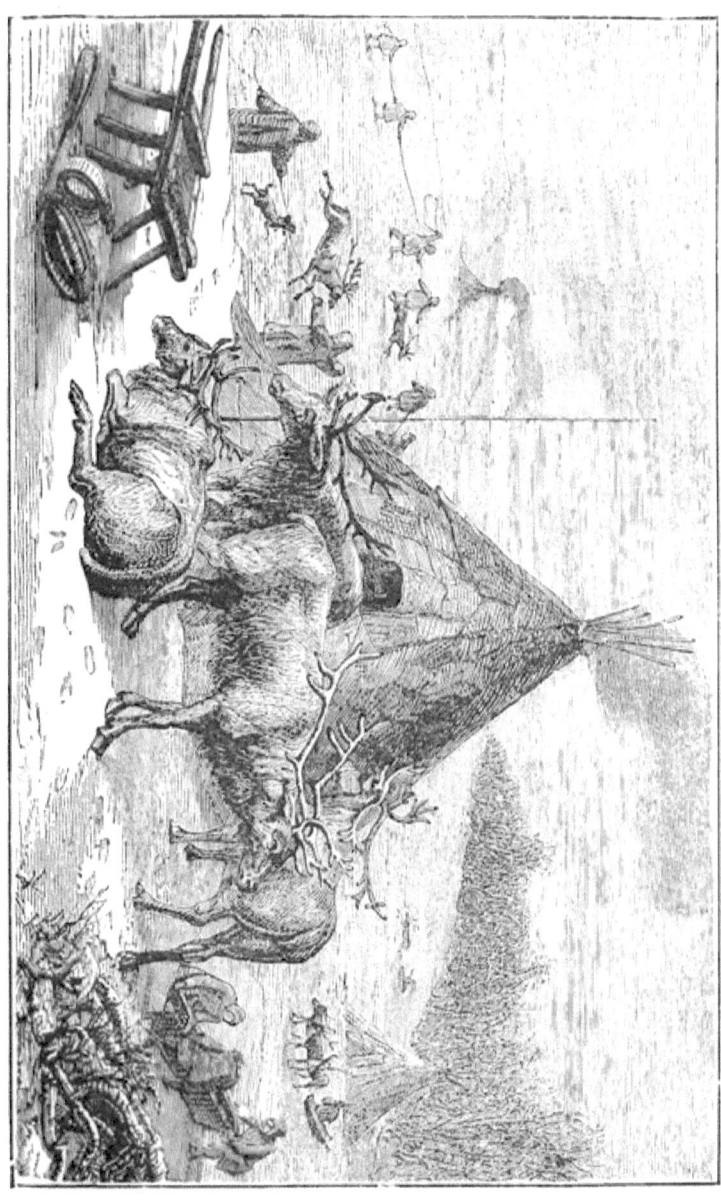

SAMOYEDE ENCAMPMENT.

and strong. Their eyes and hair are black, but their prominent and well-shaped noses distinguish them at once from their Mongolian neighbours, and are strongly suggestive of Semitic relationship.

Closely associated with the Tartars of this region, but quite distinct from them, are tribes of another aboriginal people—the Samoyedes. They are a stunted race, and their round flat faces, with black hair and eyes, plainly indicate their Mongolian affinities. Within the last few years grave mounds have been discovered near the upper waters of the Yenisei, and from these mounds various remains of the Bronze period have been unearthed, together with a number of what are believed to be Runic inscriptions. These relics most probably belong to the ancestors of the modern Samoyedes, who have many traditional references to this region as the early home of their race. The Tartars who are now settled there must have conquered and expelled them, and since that time the history of the Samoyedes has been one of continual degeneration and impoverishment. Once not only successful agriculturalists, with a very effective system of artificial irrigation, but enterprising miners and skilful workers in bronze and gold, they have quite lost the arts of their ancient civilization. They still cling to the superstitions of Shamanism; but their character is marked by a degree of firmness and independence, and they have the reputation of being honest and hospitable. Most of them are extremely poor, and they are made still poorer by the avarice of Russian and Tartar traders; while their fondness for ardent spirits, and the ravages of smallpox, are reducing their numbers more and more, and threaten their speedy extermination.

Before I reached the Obi River I had hired for this journey not less than 360 horses. Upon the whole they served me well, and for axles broken, wheels off, horses down, and other accidents, the blame may justly rest on the bad roads, dark nights, and furious driving. But, however good the horses, I had by this time had quite enough of this kind of travel, and was more than ready for a change.

Westward of Marinsk—the second town I had seen since leaving the Yenisei—our road lay through a beautiful country, not wild like the taiga, but suggestive of old parks in England—broad grassy spaces, backed by bossy woods, and cut by winding streams. Then again we entered upon a stretch of treeless steppe, and at about two o'clock one fine June morning the yemschik pulled up at a post-station right on the brink of a steep descent to what appeared to be an interminable plain. In the dim twilight I could see that the slope, and the adjoining portion of the land below, were covered with houses, and I knew at once before the yemschik told me that this was Tomsk: I knew it, and was glad, for here the long ordeal of tarantass-riding was at an end.

EXILES.

CHAPTER XI

FROM TOMSK TO THE URAL MOUNTAINS, BY RIVER AND RAILWAY

TOMSK city is the capital of a government of the same name, and which covers an area equal to one and a half times that of France. It is a region of most diversified contour. To the south is a mountainous country, with snow-clad peaks 1200 feet in height, gorges filled with glaciers, and open valleys of most fertile soil, either already under cultivation, or persuasively inviting it by the beauty and fragrance of its flora and the general luxuriance of its vegetable life. Around the bases of the mountains to the northward spreads an undulating plateau 200 miles in breadth, and upwards of 1000 feet above the level of the sea. Its surface is mostly steppe-land, and comparatively treeless; but around its numerous lakes there is rich pasturage, and extensive tracts are under cultivation. To the northward of the steppe are the lowlands around the Obi River, continuous with the swampy tundra which skirts the Arctic seas. The transition from one region to another is abrupt. As there is a sudden fall from the peaks of the

Altai Mountains to the plateau, so the plateau itself falls suddenly away by a steep declivity to the level of the north-western plains.

The city of Tomsk lies just on the margin of the lowland, hugging a portion of the western foot of the ascent to the plateau, so that in approaching it from the east—open as is the surrounding country—one cannot see the city until quite close to it. There is nothing, moreover, to indicate the direction in which it lies except the road, and, as this is a mere track across the steppe which a fall of snow may obliterate, a traveller may be within an hour's walk of the city and yet lose his way hopelessly. During the previous winter a party of nearly a hundred returning emigrants and soldiers thus met their death, the frozen corpses of some of them being found within three miles of the suburbs of the city.

This city is, after Irkutsk, the largest in Siberia, having a population of forty thousand. It has been well laid out, and, though there is nothing striking in its streets, the appearance of the whole city, with its white houses and numerous churches, as seen from the brow of the steppe above it, is both cheerful and imposing. The river Ushaika, spanned by a well-made bridge, runs through the middle of the city to join the Tom, a fine navigable river, which can be seen winding through the plain beyond the western suburbs on its way to the still larger Obi.

By far the largest building, or rather series of buildings, in Tomsk, is the university—the only one in Siberia. It was opened in 1889. The buildings had been

PART OF THE MARKET SQUARE, TOMSK.

completed long before, but the Government was so afraid
of the heresies and treasons which might possibly be bred
and nurtured there, that years were required to screw up
its courage to the risk of permitting the inauguration of a
Siberian university. Further delay was occasioned by the
difficulty of obtaining professors. There appears to be
such a widespread horror of Siberia among educated
Russians, that suitable men could not be obtained for
the various chairs except by offering larger salaries than
those connected with similar positions in St. Petersburg.
Even to obtain students, the regulations had to be made
much less stringent than those of universities in
European Russia. The medical faculty is at present the
most completely equipped.

Almost all the various industries of Siberia are
represented in the government of Tomsk; its rivers
abound with fish, and its forests with game; in the hilly
regions of the south there is mining for gold and silver
and precious stones; in the wide valleys farmers have
tens of thousands of acres of fertile land under cultivation;
and other settlers rear great herds of horses and cattle on
the plains. The wealth thus acquired enriches the
provincial city, whose importance as a mercantile centre is
greatly enhanced by its situation between the water-way
to the Ural Mountains and the post-road to the Eastern
provinces. For six months in the year, by the Obi and
its tributary the Irtish, several lines of steamers run
between Tiumen (the terminus of the Ural Mountains
Railway) and this city, which is therefore a convenient

market for the exchange of European and Siberian merchandise. As it is at Tomsk where emigrants and travellers usually commence their land journey to the East, there is a great demand for carriages, and as many as fifty thousand sledges and tarantasses are manufactured in the city every year.

The voyage from Tomsk to the Ural Mountains usually occupies a week, but the steamer by which I took passage had a barge in tow, and did not therefore progress so rapidly. But we had the current with us, and a couple of hours after leaving had reached the mouth of the Tom River, and saw around us the broader waters of the Obi. The elevated table-land and bordering hills soon sank below the horizon, and we had on every side of us the beginning of the great northern plains. The country was so flat that we could see nothing beyond the river-banks, which were covered with forest to the water's edge, and, at the distance of our steamer, seemed only like serrated bands of green and purple separating the expanse of water from the sky.

In the Tom River we saw a dozen sturdy Russians with a long tow-line hauling a large cargo-boat up towards the city, just as Chinese boatmen do when working against wind and current. Near the junction of this river with the Obi was an immense raft of pine-logs, which was being ingeniously carried up the stream by means of a cable, one end of which was attached to an anchor fixed half a mile or so ahead, and the other to a capstan worked by four horses on the fore-part of the raft. When the raft had

STEAMER TOWING BARGE.

nearly reached the anchor, a second one, with another length of cable, was sent ahead in a small boat, and, as soon as it was fixed at the required distance, the horses began again to turn the capstan. A still larger raft was seen a few hours later; it must have measured from six to eight hundred feet in length, and had a capstan with four horses at each end.

After the first day we saw neither rafts nor boats of any kind. Every hundred miles we stopped at a lonely wood-station to take in fuel, and generally from one wood-station to another was an unbroken solitude. Little groups of islands here and there appeared, and sometimes we saw smaller tributary rivers flowing into ours; but, apart from these, there was nothing but the increasing broadness of the river to indicate that we were not to-day passing precisely the same place we passed yesterday.

At one wood-station, where our steamer was moored for the night, I had an opportunity of visiting a camp of Ostiaks—another interesting tribe of Siberian aborigines, once very numerous in the country, but now rapidly succumbing to the ravages of vodka and the venom of Russian sensuality.

Some of these Ostiaks are working as agriculturalists upon the southern steppes; others, scattered over the northern tundra, keep herds of reindeer; but the purest specimens of the race are those engaged in fishing on the Obi. They are a diminutive people, the average height of the men being about five feet, and that of the women six inches less. They have dark-brown hair, small eyes, broad flat noses, thick lips, and scanty beard. Their clothing consisted of trousers, tunics, and mocassins of reindeer skin; and they lived in huts of birch-bark, some of them conical in shape, like an Indian wigwam.

Birch-bark is not only used by the Ostiaks for housebuilding; beaten until it is soft and supple, it serves them for blankets and outer garments; and whatever baskets, milk basins, and clothes-boxes they have are made of the same material. The inner, smooth surface of the bark, which forms the outside of the boxes, is often ornamented with quaint lines and figures, which have evidently been burnt into the tissue with a red-hot piece of iron or stone. Some of these boxes, about a foot in length, and very neatly made, were offered for sale at what some of my fellow-passengers considered the exorbitant price of ten kopeks, or 2½d. each.

It is said of the Ostiaks, by those who know them well, that, in spite of the hardships of their life, they are honest and kind; and from the little I saw of them, I can well believe that such praise is deserved. Their religion, like that of most other native races in Siberia, is Shamanism. Efforts have again and again been made to convert them to Christianity, or rather something has been done with this end in view; it hardly amounts to effort. Simple as is the life of a Siberian priest, he could not, without a good deal of self-denial, spend any considerable length of time among such people as the Ostiaks; and therefore, if ordered by his bishop to go and convert a tribe of them, he contents himself with making a bonfire of their idols, administering the rite of baptism, and distributing some small silver coins.

When the priest has left them, the poor, uninstructed people, feeling lonely without their fetiches, begin at once to manufacture new ones. There is no time for elaborate carving, so, getting an ordinary board, they burn with a hot iron, upon one end of it, the rough image of a face—eyes, nose, and mouth; and this serves as their mediating divinity, the link between themselves and the spirit-world, until a priest happens to come round again.

The great defect in the missionary agencies of Russia, as indeed in all the ministrations of the State Church itself, is the lack of instruction. The ritual of the Church is believed to be sufficient, and an intelligent conception of the spiritual meaning of the rites a matter of very subordinate importance.

Converts are being slowly made among the Buriats of the Trans-Baikal province; but the only great success I have heard of in connection with the missionary operations of the Russian Church is the conversion of the Tartar tribes upon the Lena. The method adopted in this case, though so successful, is hardly likely to commend itself to the missionary societies of Britain, but it illustrates the Russian notion of evangelism, and shows not only a shrewd knowledge of human nature, but a readiness to take advantage of its weaknesses. Instead of sending a band of missionaries to live among them, and lead them step by step into the light of Christian truth, a decree of State was passed, and transmitted by Imperial messenger, informing these Lena Tartars that, in recognition of their loyalty and good behaviour, the Czar had by special edict graciously conceded to them the privilege of being admitted to the Imperial Church; that a band of instructors was on the way to prepare them for the initiatory rites; and that, at any early date, such of them as had profited by their instruction would be baptized.

The bait was successful. The Tartars felt themselves so flattered by this mark of the Czar's favour, that the whole tribe applied for admission to the Church.

As we proceeded northward the June days lengthened until, when we had passed the latitude of 60°, there was no night at all. The sun just dipped below the horizon, but the sunset glory never faded, and as banners waving above hedgerows indicate the progress of an unseen procession, so the golden splendours of the evening followed the sun's movement round the north until again they brightened into day. Because there was no darkness, we seemed for a while to become oblivious of the time, whether of day or night. Walking up and down on the shore at a wood-station one day, I found it was two o'clock in the morning. Not having been accustomed since infancy to go to bed by daylight, I was waiting for the familiar curtains to be drawn. When I woke and called for breakfast it was afternoon, and all the rest of my fellow-passengers were still asleep.

The confluence of the Obi with the Irtish was the limit of our voyage northward, and turning into the latter river we began to steam again towards the south.

The Irtish, though smaller than the Obi, is a magnificent river, running a course of 2500 miles, three-fourths of which is navigable. The scenery around the lower portions of its course is similar to that upon the Obi—bright water and blue sky, with an intervening strip of low forest-covered bank; but, the river being confined in a narrower channel, the trees on either side, and any bit of rising ground, seem much larger, and do more to relieve the flatness of the landscape.

The current was against us now, and, having the broad, heavy-laden barge in tow, our speed was considerably slackened. But we never stopped except to take in fuel, and on the fourth day after entering the Irtish we turned from it into the River Tobol, which soon brought us to the city of Tobolsk. It had been in sight for several hours before we reached it, the river here running a very winding course, and the city being made conspicuous by its situation on the top of an isolated crag—a peculiar rocky platform, which rises two hundred feet above the surrounding plain.

Tobolsk is the oldest city in Siberia, dating from the middle of the reign of our Queen Elizabeth, and it has an ancient, settled look. The population does not exceed fifteen thousand, and is not increasing; but the streets being wide, and separated from one another by open spaces of grass-land, the city occupies a large area, spreading itself out beyond the surface of the rock, to cover, with its poorer suburbs, most of the flat between it and the river.

In going from the steamer to the centre of the town

we passed through busy streets of little open-fronted shops, where small traders—many of them Jews—offered for sale various kinds of Siberian produce, among which was a very miscellaneous assortment of tanned and untanned skins. The side-walks are paved with planks, which bend and rattle beneath our feet, and look so worn that they cannot be very frequently renewed. In the middle of the city is a square, one side of which is occupied by an immense prison with accommodation for two thousand prisoners. It is chiefly used as a place of temporary detention for exiles on their way to the East.

One of the strangest exiles ever sent out to Siberia has been located for more than two centuries in this city—the bell of the church at Uglitch, and which had the audacity to ring an alarm when Boris Godunoff, to secure for himself the throne, was accomplishing the murder of his nephew the Czarowitch Dmitri.

Around these emblems of the rigorous government of an autocratic Czar, twenty-one churches and two cathedrals remind the people of the overruling power of God. Mental culture is by no means disregarded, for the city has in its museum a good collection of aboriginal implements, natural history specimens, and paleontological remains. There are also several educational establishments of good repute; and most of the girls' schools in Siberia are indebted for their teachers to the Marie Training Institution of Tobolsk.

This city does a considerable trade in timber and salt fish, but its commercial importance depends mainly on its

TOBOLSK.

corn market; and the small and comparatively stationary number of inhabitants in what was once the capital of Siberia, and is still the chief city of its most populous province, arises from the fact that by far the larger portion of the settlers are engaged in agricultural pursuits. It could not easily be otherwise, for the vast province of Tobolsk, with an area equal to at least six times that of Great Britain, consists almost entirely of alluvial plains, the only exceptions being the rocky northern extremity of the Ural Mountains, and a few such lonely crags as that upon which this city stands.

The great plain which we saw on either side the river, and which is known as the Tobol Steppe, comprises twenty-five millions of acres of rich black soil, and is one of the most fertile tracts of country in the world. Of the one and a half millions of people in the province of Tobolsk, about one million are settled on this steppe; and the district is said to be more characteristically Russian than the plains on the banks of the Volga.

The climate is trying to the settlers, but not detrimental to the crops, for, though the winters are terribly severe, the sun in the summer shines through the clear, dry atmosphere with such unusual power, that wheat and other cereals come to maturity with a rapidity which would astonish Western cultivators. The area now under tillage on this steppe amounts to about three and a half millions of acres, by far the greater part of its fertile surface still waiting for the plough. There are other steppes of similar fertility, and almost equal size; and the total arable surface of this province is so extensive, that if only half of it were utilized, enough wheat could be produced to supply all Europe with bread.

These fertile steppes are in the southern half of the Tobolsk government; farther north we passed through a very different region—a region still of alluvial soil, but spread out in those vast quivering morasses which form the dreadful *urmans* of Siberia. For hundreds of miles this region is covered with forest; gigantic cedars, larches, pines, crowded together in the marsh, the space between them filled with such dense growths of underwood that even in the winter, when hard frost gives solid standing-ground, without a hatchet to clear the way, progress is impossible.

Outside the forest areas are immense level tracts of open country covered with a grassy carpet of the tenderest green, varied by flowery patches of white, and gold, and pink, and purple, and all so smooth, and fresh, and beautiful, as if inviting the traveller to wander there. But such invitation is a delusion and a snare. Only in the winter can these flowery meads be visited, and then they are no longer flowery; but to attempt to traverse them in summer, except with special apparatus, means being sucked down alive into the grave.

Even to wild animals these urmans are forbidden ground. The nimble-stepping, broad-hoofed reindeer can sometimes cross them safely in the summer-time, but most other large animals attempting to do so would quickly be engulphed, and this may be a partial explanation of the remains of mammoth and rhinoceros which are so abundant and so widely diffused through these northern marshlands of Siberia.

In the museum here at Tobolsk are numerous specimens of mammoth, and throughout this region they are by no means rare. When an ice-pack breaks down a river-bank, or floods tear up a frozen marsh, or the summer thaw penetrates a little more deeply than usual into the ground, some of these antediluvian monsters are sure to be exposed. In many cases they are so fresh and well preserved, with their dark shaggy hair and underwool of reddish brown, their tufted ears and long curved tusks, that all the aborigines, and even some of the Russian settlers, persist in the belief that they are specimens of animals which still live, burrowing under ground like moles, and which die the instant they are admitted to the light.

The farther one goes northward the more abundant do these remains become. They are washed up with every tide upon the Arctic shores, and some extensive islands off the coast seem to consist almost entirely of fossil ivory and bones. Tusks which have been long or repeatedly exposed to the air are brittle and unserviceable, but those which have remained buried in the ice retain the qualities of recent ivory, and are a valuable article of merchandise. There is a great market for these mammoth tusks at Yakutsk, on the Lena, from which they find their way not only to the workshops of European Russia, but even to the ivory carvers of Canton.

Various trinkets and works of art are made of these remains, and are sold at the shops, and especially at the museum of Tobolsk, as mementos of a visit to this graveyard of the mammoth. One of the favourite curios very accurately resembled a slice of Russian bread and cheese. But the bread was really a transverse section of one of the long bones of a mammoth, and the cheese was a piece of ivory from his tusk; the two thus joined together being sold at a price which enabled the ingenious contriver to obtain for himself many times their weight of the homely fare they simulated.

This paludal region of Tobolsk is not altogether uninhabited. Ostiak hunters roam over it in winter in search of pelts, and even in summer a few of them contrive, with something like snow-shoes on their feet, to penetrate for twenty or thirty miles into these swampy wilds. I saw one day a pair of wild swans rise from the water, near the mouth of the Irtish, and sail far away over the marshes. As from time to time they stretched their long necks to inspect the country over which they flew, they must sometimes have seen human dwellers there, and with eyes so keen as theirs have recognised that they were not Ostiaks, but white-faced Europeans.

For some of the best of Russian Nonconformists, goaded to distraction by oppression, and wishful both to be true to their convictions and to preserve their liberty, have, by toilsome winter explorations, discovered patches of dry land in these swamps, and, joined by such of their relatives and friends as were like-minded, bringing with them a few cattle and bushels of seed-corn, here they have settled with their families, and, protected by these impenetrable wastes of urman, fear no more either the eye of the informer or the hand of arbitrary power. Only the wild swans know where they are, and they will tell no tales.

Three new passengers joined us at Tobolsk—young men of about twenty years of age—sons of Russian settlers at Omsk, and who, having completed their course at the gymnasium, were now on their way to the University of St. Petersburg. If they were at all typical of the educated youth of Russia, the prospects of the empire are bright. While frank, honest, and light-hearted, they had the reverence which taught them to take their shoes off their feet when approaching holy ground. By no means deficient in intelligence or manly independence, they yet showed none of that superciliousness on the one hand, nor of morbid self-consciousness upon the other, which mar the disposition of so many of the same class of young men in England.

One of them played the violin with rare taste and proficiency, and all three were aspiring vocalists — if aspiring be an appropriate word to represent their evident desire to reach a lower note than any other bass singer in the world. The first thing in the morning, the last at night, and many times during the day, one or another of them might be heard and seen attempting to run or rumble down the gamut—deeper and yet deeper still, from a groan to a roar, from this to distant thunder, and then a fall to vocal depths which were quite inaudible; the only sign that the singer was still singing being his attitude and his grimace.

A voyage of three days up the Tobol brought us to its confluence with the Toora, a small navigable river which runs down from the Ural Mountains. The river systems of Siberia are remarkable for their numerous confluences, and the facilities for inland navigation thus afforded explain the wide dissemination throughout the country of Russian settlements. With the exception of the Amoor, all the great rivers of Siberia run from south to north, but each of them is formed by the union of two other navigable rivers; and the course of a Siberian river system, as shown upon a map, may be roughly represented by an inverted Y. Each of these confluent rivers receives its own navigable tributaries, the general direction of whose course is east and west,—and thus regions, not only far apart, but in all sorts of directions, are brought into communication; so that at certain seasons of the year, with a suitable boat, the whole of Siberia might be crossed from the Pacific Ocean to the Ural Mountains, with only a few days' interval of land travel.

The present voyage commenced upon the River Tom, from the Tom we passed into the Obi, from the Obi to the Irtish, from the Irtish to the Tobol, and, last of all, from the Tobol to the Toora—travelling for considerable distances up or down these five rivers without a single change of steamer.

A fine country lay around us as we steamed up the Toora River. Farmsteads and villages were continually in sight, surrounded by cultivated fields, or tracts of meadowland on which large numbers of cattle and horses, and sometimes sheep, were grazing; and there was nothing but the architecture of the churches to remind us that we were not in some of the rural districts of Western Europe.

The barge we had in tow was left behind in the Tobol, so we made more rapid progress now; and towards the end of June, two days after entering the Toora, and twelve days after leaving Tomsk, we finished our voyage at the city of Tiumen.

The river here is about as wide as the Thames at Richmond. On its left or northern bank is a low-lying plain, covered near the river with the huts of the poorer settlers. A bridge connects this district with the city, which lies on the south side of the river, covering the slopes of a somewhat steep ascent to the plateau and a considerable area of the plateau itself. Most of the houses are built of wood, but they look neat and comfortable, and many of them are surrounded by gardens.

This city is almost as old as Tobolsk, and has not only a larger population, but its citizens are reputed to be the best-looking people in the country. But this does not mean much; for however kind and honest and intelligent and persevering the people of Siberia may be, an unprejudiced observer can hardly overlook the fact that nature seems to have fashioned their features into harmony with the rugged aspects of the country in which they live.

As a trading city, Tiumen is only outrivalled by Irkutsk and Tomsk, and the enterprising industry of its inhabitants have made it an important manufacturing centre. It has the only paper mill in the country. The coarse carpets woven in this city are finding their way as Oriental curiosities into the markets of the West. There are over a hundred tanneries, and Tiumen leather is found in all parts of the country; but a considerable number of the hides prepared here are used in the town itself, which turns out every year not less than seventy thousand pairs of top-boots and three hundred thousand pairs of leather gloves.

But to emigrants and travellers Tiumen is chiefly interesting as the first place of embarkation on the navigable rivers of Siberia, and the eastern terminus of the railway across the Ural Mountains. The station is two miles distant from the town, and is an imposing building of red brick, much too large for the requirements of present traffic, which is limited to one arrival and one departure every twenty-four hours.

Our train left a little before midnight, and it took us, even by railway, two nights and a day to reach the Kama River, on the western side of the range. It was tantalizing to commence this journey in the dark,—being impatient for a look at the mighty range of mountains which have been the scene of so many romantic stories. Information received in later days had tended to abate, or to destroy, the awe with which one had been taught to think of the Ural Mountains, but I still half-expected to see something of the dreadful precipices, dizzy heights, wild gorges, and gloomy caverns of which I had so often heard.

Nothing could be seen from the train, for the night

was dark, and the lights in the carriage made the outside darker still; so at length, tired of looking, I fell into a sound sleep, and did not wake again until after dawn. Sure of having a good view of the Urals now, I hastened to the outside platform at the end of the carriage, but it appeared that we had not reached the mountains yet, for whichever way I looked I could see nothing of them. What I did see, as I sat and watched, was a forest of fir-trees, with dense undergrowth of bushes, close up to the line on either side, and, at intervals of half a dozen miles or more, a quaint little wooden station, looking smaller than it was because of the tall cedars which stood round it. Then came a break in the forest, and the line passed through rolling plains of luxuriant grass-land, sloping down gently here and there into a hollow through which some peaceful river flowed, its waters almost hidden sometimes by the groves of willow, alder, and wild cherry on its banks; and then the shadow of the forest fell upon the line again.

Some rain had fallen in the night, and the vegetation had enjoyed it, as the beauty and freshness of its many shades of green this morning showed. There was plenty of interesting scenery, but no Ural Mountains. I strained my neck out of the window to look ahead, but there was nothing between the verdure and the sky.

Having another twenty-four hours of railway ride before us, I comforted myself with the reflection that we should reach the awful mountains by and by; but soon we approached a busy town, and as our train drew up at the station I saw with astonishment that it was Ekaterinburg—a town which is represented on the map as being only 350 feet below the summit of the range.

"Where are the Ural Mountains?" exclaimed a fellow-passenger of whom I had ventured to inquire. "Why, unless you have been looking at the sky, you have seen nothing else all day."

The Ural chain of mountains is a long one, and its northern and southern extremities may be as wild and rugged as ancient descriptions represent, but the Middle Urals, which we crossed, are simply broad, unbroken swellings of the earth, and, though they attain in one place an altitude of over 4000 feet, they reach it by a slope too gentle to be perceptible. We must perform a railway journey equal to half the length of England to gain an elevation of 1000 feet, and in no place, to the eye of the observer, can the mountain-side be distinguished from an undulating plain.

This region has great attractions for the Russians in its fertile soil and mineral wealth, and spread over the slopes of the Middle Urals are nearly two million settlers. All the platinum and one-fifth of the gold produced in the whole empire are obtained in this region; and the 103 blast-furnaces between Ekaterinburg and Perm supply two-thirds of all the pig-iron manufactured in the country. Copper also is abundant, and here at Ekaterinburg the Government has a mint for making copper coin.

This city is one of the most important centres of the Ural mining industry. It is well built, occupying both sides of the River Isset, and has a population of nearly thirty thousand. The railway affords a good view of it,

A STREET IN EKATERINBURG.

and its look of prosperity and comfort is not deceptive, for with its numerous churches, substantial houses, schools, hospitals, orphanage, and museum, it will compare favourably with any European city of equal size.

In addition to the mint, the Government has a factory here for cutting and polishing jasper, malachite, porphyry, and other ornamental stones which are met with near the city. Many of the working people increase their income by doing a little of this kind of work on their own account. The women and children go out and find the stones, and, when they have been carved into the shape of polar bears, wolves, reindeer, and various domestic animals, the women and children take charge again, and walk up and down the platform of the railway station, or about the streets, seeking purchasers for these specimens of Ekaterinburg produce and handicraft. Emeralds, amethysts, and other precious stones are also found in the neighbourhood of the city; and connected with the railway station is a stall, at which Ural jewellery, mounted in rings and brooches of Ural gold, may be bought at reasonable prices.

What we saw of Ekaterinburg had to be accomplished quickly, for after little more than an hour's delay our train went on again. The scenery was similar to that which we had already passed—woodland, meadows, cultivated fields; but no appearance anywhere of mountains, nor even of elevated ground, and we did not pass a single tunnel, not even deep cutting, in the whole distance between Tiumen and Perm.

But we were continually ascending, and in the late

evening twilight stopped at a small station bearing the great name of "Asia." After a short run beyond it we reached a precisely similar station, called "Europe." Both stations were built in lonely spots, the few dwellings in their neighbourhood being probably occupied by people connected with the line; but these two groups of workmen's houses are supposed to be the nuclei of future townships called by these high-sounding names.

They are not merely names. "Asia" is a Siberian village, on the continent of Asia, and must bear the burden of the heavier charges for telegrams and postage which it pleases the Russian Government to impose upon its Siberian subjects. "Europe," though only two miles distant, is a European village, and has all the privileges associated with the name.

Midway between these two stations is a marble pillar, of triangular section, which has been erected as a landmark by the Government, and so placed that the apex of the triangle lies upon the line of that parting of the waters which indicates the summit of the Ural range. Any spring of water bursting from the ground eastward of that line will flow down the eastern slope and connect itself with the river systems of Siberia; a spring to the westward will as surely find its way down the western slope to join some European river. This line of the parting of the waters, therefore, is also the boundary line between the continents; and so the marble pillar bears, on one of the two sides adjacent to its apex, the name "Asia," and on the other "Europe." When that pillar was behind me I knew that I had completed my journey across Siberia.

THE SIBERIAN BOUNDARY POST.

CHAPTER XII

CROSSING THE RUSSIAN FRONTIER

WHATEVER dangers, either to liberty or life, may be associated with travel in Siberia, it seemed natural enough to think that, having entered Europe, these were passed. But the Russians are suspicious of strangers, especially of strangers from the East, and I was not yet as safe as I supposed.

Within the confines of the Czar's dominion there was no interference with my movements. Sailing on the Kama and the Volga Rivers, and strolling through the booths of the great fair at Nijni Novgorod, or round the Kreml at Moscow, or about the streets and bridges of St. Petersburg, I was free—as free as a bird is in its cage. The cage was in this case a big one—as big as the Russian Empire; but, like all other cages, it presented to its inmates on every side impassable barriers and bolted doors.

The Russian Government has no doubt some excuse for the strictness of its laws, and the close espionage under which its subjects are compelled to live. It is no easy task to control such a great and heterogeneous population —Mongols, Tartars, Finns, and Jews intermixed, but unassimilated with the Slavonic people; and not in Siberia only, for there are large communities of Mohammedan Tartars, and even of Mongol Kalmucks, in the very heart of European Russia. It is easier and more usual for one tribe to learn the vices of another than its virtues, and this may account, in some degree, for the peculiarly desperate character of Russian criminals.

But it is impossible to have different sets of laws for each separate tribe, and equally impossible for a despotic ruler to restrain effectually the evil passions of the bad without imposing irksome restrictions upon the good. The meshes of a net must have their size regulated by the kind of fish we wish to catch; and the penal laws of Russia, expressly made to hinder crime, appear to be based on the assumption that it is better to let ten who are innocent be punished than one who is guilty escape. But Russia is growing fast, and she can hardly fail to learn from these experiments, as other Governments have learned before, that the evils of license are less to be dreaded than those of tyrannical repression, and that only in an atmosphere of liberty can those virtues flourish which make a country truly great.

I took a through-ticket from Wilna to the nearest town in Germany, and after a five hours' run our train reached the little frontier station of Wirballen. We had to wait here half an hour while passports were examined, and detectives made a careful survey of the passengers, lest anyone under the suspicion of the authorities should slip out of their hands.

It afforded some diversion to watch the process of inspection, and I was more amused than frightened at the attention which some of the detectives paid to me. Then they retired to consult, and soon after a couple of soldiers and an officer were seen advancing towards the train. Evidently, some suspect had been discovered. As the men were approaching directly towards my carriage, I looked round searchingly at my fellow-passengers, wondering which of them it could be, and was not a little astonished when the soldiers came straight up to me, and, seizing my baggage, told me to get out of the train. As soon as I had alighted on the platform, the guard gave his signal to the engine-driver, and the train moved off.

The captain who had ordered my arrest was a cultured and gentlemanly officer, and he treated me with as much courtesy as was possible under the circumstances. As my passport had been submitted to the inspection of Russian officers in every city, town, and village at which I had rested for an hour, from one end of the empire to the other, I was not surprised at his admission that it was not in any way irregular. He would not compromise himself, nor hurt my feelings, by definitely stating the nature and grounds of his suspicion, but would merely say that I had come from Siberia, that my dress and my general appearance told him so apart from my frank confession, and that there were circumstances in the case which made it his duty to detain me until he had received instructions from headquarters at St. Petersburg.

The soldiers were not so reticent. They plainly told

me that I was not an Englishman, but a Russian; that my blundering way of speaking the language was a pretence; that there was reason to believe me to be an escaped exile; and that the passport produced by me had no doubt been taken from some traveller whom I had murdered. When I innocently called attention to other proofs of my identity—a banker's letter of credit, visiting cards, pocket-book, and correspondence—the soldiers gave a knowing chuckle, and replied, that of course when I took the passport from the traveller I took his other papers too.

Wirballen, or, as the Russians call it, Verzhbolovo, is only a small village, and most of its inhabitants are either persons employed on the railway, or Government officials. The surrounding country consists of meadow-land and corn-fields, dotted here and there with farmhouses and clumps of trees. I had to sleep in the waiting-room at the railway station, but was allowed to walk about freely in the neighbourhood of the village, though no doubt under continual observation. No food was provided; and as my stock of Russian currency was running low, and could not be easily replenished in a village too small to possess a bank, I had to exercise the most rigid economy, and be content with the homeliest fare. Having purchased a big loaf of bread, a slice from it whenever I felt hungry enough to appreciate such wholesome dietary, with a drink of water from a spring, had to serve me for my daily meals.

I went out one day to a little farmhouse near the village in the hope of being able to procure some milk, but

rumours had got afloat of the dangerous character who had
been arrested here, and the people were afraid. Several
women were moving about in the farmyard when first I
turned towards it, but the place was quite deserted when
I arrived, and, though I knocked at the door and shouted
for a quarter of an hour, no one ventured to appear.

The same evening, towards dusk, when walking quietly
along a country lane, I saw three gentlemen approaching.
They were dressed as if going to a party, and were engaged
in such earnest conversation that they did not notice me
until they had approached within a dozen yards, when all
at once, as if panic-struck, they scrambled up the bank
into the fields.

One morning I strolled on to the highway which
crosses the frontier into Germany. The boundary line
between the two countries is marked by a deep, narrow,
grass-covered gully, at the bottom of which is a ditch. A
small wooden bridge connects the two banks, but beyond
the bridge on the German side I could see nothing, the
road turning abruptly to the left behind a mass of
shrubbery and trees.

A soldier was guarding the Russian end of the bridge,
and there were other soldiers in the house beside it.
Market women, with baskets on their arm, were crossing
in one direction or the other frequently. Each one
showed her passport to the soldier and went on; but, as
soon as I was spied upon the road, an alarm was given,
and several soldiers with fixed bayonets stood out across
the entrance to the bridge. They had evidently been

warned that I might attempt to get across the frontier with a rush. The span of the bridge was only about thirty feet, and if I could reach the other side of it I should be free; but it would be madness for anyone whose life is not already forfeited to face the risks of such a rush. "I only want to look at the bridge," I said. "But you cannot be allowed to look," the officer in charge replied, "and must at once go off this road."

Not being sufficiently interested in the skilful marksmanship of Russian soldiers to lend myself as a target for their rifle-practice, I retraced my steps.

Life in Wirballen was becoming somewhat monotonous. I had watched the coming and going of the trains at the station, explored every street and alley of the village, and there appeared to be no interesting occupation left. But when I asked permission to return to St. Petersburg or some other Russian town, they told me in reply, that if I would be patient for a few days longer I should probably find myself on my way back to Siberia.

The British Embassy at St. Petersburg, in reply to a telegram of mine, returned a prompt promise of assistance; but the Russian police insisted upon such a complete investigation, extending as far back as the remotest Siberian settlements, that, though the inquiries were made by telegraph, they involved a considerable expenditure of time; and it was not until the evening of the third day that the captain informed me, by a note in French, that a message had just arrived from St. Petersburg ordering my release, and that I was at liberty to cross the frontier whenever I wished.

Naturally, I wished to do it there and then: if the cage-door is open, the sooner one gets outside the better, lest it should close again. As no train was leaving for the West until the following morning, I hired a cart, and at once set out for the German railway station at Eydtkuhnen. As we turned into the road which leads to the frontier, the sentry at the bridge again gave the alarm, and the soldiers ran out from the house to block the passage. Waving the captain's letter in my hand, I told the driver to go on, but we were forced to stop at a considerable distance from the bridge while the letter was examined. It was passed from one to another, and they all declared it to be a forgery. In vain I protested, and in vain the driver helped me. The only favour the soldiers could be persuaded to allow, was to let one of their number go with me to the captain for a verbal confirmation of the note.

A soldier joined me in the cart, and back we went to the town again. The delay was vexing, and all the more so because I had hoped to catch a train which was that night leaving the German station for Berlin. But this was not the last of my vexations. In springing from the cart at the captain's residence a projecting nail caught the soldier's trousers and gave them an ugly tear, so the man sprang back again into the cart, made the driver move on a few hundred paces, and declared that he would not present himself before the captain until his torn garment was repaired. The carter borrowed a needle and thread from a roadside cottage; and while I endeavoured, with indifferent success, to look on with equanimity, the soldier proceeded deliberately to stitch up the long rent. Then we went in to see the captain.

He did not, of course, repudiate his letter, so we were soon on our way to the bridge once more. There I had to wait for half an hour while the officer in charge took a copy of my passport, and wrote out a description of my dress and appearance. Then I received permission to proceed; and when the hollow beat of the horse's hoofs upon the bridge told me that I was outside the cage at last, I felt inclined to give expression to my feelings by an English cheer. But just then, at the bend of the road, I was confronted by two tall German soldiers, and for a few moments seemed in danger of being a sort of shuttlecock between the keepers of the two ends of the bridge.

But as soon as the German soldiers knew my nationality they handed back my passport, would not trouble me to open my portmanteau, said that, if I had come across Siberia, I must have had already my full share of annoyances; and, telling the carter to drive on, they shouted after me their wish that I might have a quick and pleasant journey home to England.

And so I had.

www.ingramcontent.com/pod-product-compliance
Lightning Source LLC
Chambersburg PA
CBHW021357230426
43666CB00006B/557